Hockey Drills for Passing & Receiving

George Gwozdecky
University of Denver

Vern Stenlund
University of Windsor

Human Kinetics

Library of Congress Cataloging-in-Publication Data

Gwozdecky, George, 1953-
    Hockey drills for passing & receiving / by George Gwozdecky, Vern Stenlund.
      p. cm.
    ISBN 0-7360-0004-6
    1. Hockey--Training.   I. Stenlund, K. Vern.   II. Title.
III. Title: Hockey drills for passing and receiving.
GV848.3.G96   1999
796.962'2--dc21   99-22734
                                                           CIP

ISBN 0-7360-0004-6

Managing Editor: Cynthia McEntire; **Assistant Editor:** Laurie Stokoe; **Copyeditor:** Amie Bell; **Proofreader:** Lisa Satterthwaite; **Graphic Designer:** Judy Henderson; **Graphic Artist:** Francine Hamerski; **Photo Editor:** Clark Brooks; **Cover Designer:** Jack Davis; **Photographer (cover):** © SportsChrome; **Photographer (interior):** Tom Roberts, unless otherwise indicated; **Illustrators:** Argosy and Tom Roberts; **Printer:** Versa Press

Human Kinetics books are available at special discounts for bulk purchase. Special editions or book excerpts can also be created to specification. For details, contact the Special Sales Manager at Human Kinetics.

Printed in the United States of America 10 9 8 7 6 5 4 3 2 1

Human Kinetics
Web site: http://www.humankinetics.com/

United States: Human Kinetics
P.O. Box 5076
Champaign, IL 61825-5076
1-800-747-4457
e-mail: humank@hkusa.com

Canada: Human Kinetics
475 Devonshire Road Unit 100
Windsor, ON N8Y 2L5
1-800-465-7301 (in Canada only)
e-mail: humank@hkcanada.com

Europe: Human Kinetics, P.O. Box IW14
Leeds LS16 6TR, United Kingdom
+44 (0)113-278 1708
e-mail: humank@hkeurope.com

Australia: Human Kinetics
57A Price Avenue
Lower Mitcham, South Australia 5062
(08) 82771555
e-mail: humank@hkaustralia.com

New Zealand: Human Kinetics
P.O. Box 105-231, Auckland Central
09-523-3462
e-mail: humank@hknewz.com

This book is dedicated to the most important people in my life:

My wife Bonnie and daughter Adrienne for their love, patience, and understanding of a coach's life;

My father George and mother Eunice, who gave me the opportunity to pursue my dreams;

My brothers Peter and Mark, who made our growing years fun, competitive, and rewarding;

Albert Cava, my junior coach in Thunder Bay, who taught me that heart, toughness, and courage can overcome any kind of challenge;

Bob Johnson, my coach at the University of Wisconsin, whose incredible enthusiasm for hockey whet my coaching appetite and led me to my first coaching position;

My mentor at Michigan State University, Ron Mason, who assisted in the development of my teaching and coaching philosophy and taught me the principle for building a college hockey program with integrity. He always insisted on respect for the game and all of the individuals who comprise it;

And finally, my friend and confidante at Miami University, Steve Cady, who taught me that "even though you may not have the best of everything, you must make the best of everything you have."

It is impossible to express what these people have meant to me. I will forever be indebted for their invaluable gifts.

George Gwozdecky

It is always a privilege to be involved in the writing of materials such as these because the written word reflects the contributions of so many people over the years. To all the coaches that I have been blessed to work with or compete against, this one's for you. And to all the coaches who will gain even one piece of information from these pages which might impact their coaching in a positive way, this work is for you as well. Coaching, whether pee-wee or pro, is indeed a fraternity, and I feel blessed to have been a small part of it.

And finally, to Grandma Hunter, whose wisdom through the years served as a foundation for much of what would unfold in my life. Thank you, Grandma.

Vern Stenlund

Contents

Drill Finder

The Drill Finder is a reference for quick identification of the different aspects of passing and receiving incorporated into each drill. Although the drills in this book are organized within specific chapters that deal with unique aspects of passing and receiving, in many cases a drill can be used to practice other skill areas or provide more challenging practices. Remember to review the "Drill Progressions" section of each drill for ways to adapt the drill to your own objectives. By focusing on the peripheral skills included in each drill, you may find it easier to organize efficient practices using a variety of themes.

Drill #	Drill	Fundamental	Timing	Speed	Conditioning	Transitions	Advanced skills	Fun
1.	Hit the Cone	X						
2.	Stationary Passing and Receiving	X						
3.	Intercept	X						X
4.	Pepper	X	X					X
5.	Self-Serve	X	X					
6.	Passing Relay	X	X					
7.	Box Pass	X						
8.	Escalator	X	X					
9.	Full-Ice Reverse	X	X	X				
10.	The Weave	X	X	X			X	X
11.	Alternate Passing and Receiving	X	X					X
12.	Stop-and-Go Passing and Receiving	X	X	X			X	X
13.	Swing Warm-Up	X	X	X		X		
14.	Monkey in the Middle Progression	X	X					X
15.	Drexie Warm-Up	X	X	X				
16.	Mason Partner Pass	X	X					
17.	Six-Line Wave Progression	X	X					
18.	Back and Forth	X	X				X	X
19.	Stagger Passing and Receiving	X	X	X			X	
20.	Leamington Warm-Up	X	X	X	X		X	
21.	Single Wheel	X	X	X	X	X		X
22.	2-on-0 Wheel	X	X	X	X	X		X
23.	Situation Wheel	X	X	X	X	X	X	X
24.	Delayed Wheel	X	X	X	X	X	X	X
25.	Six-Pass Wheel	X	X	X	X	X	X	X
26.	Reverse Six-Pass Wheel	X	X	X	X	X	X	X
27.	Four-Corner Wheel	X	X	X	X	X	X	X
28.	Two-Puck Exchange		X	X	X	X	X	X
29.	Continuous One-Puck Wheel		X	X	X	X	X	X
30.	Russian Wheel Half-Ice		X	X	X	X	X	X
31.	Double Blues	X	X	X		X		
32.	Back It Up		X	X		X	X	
33.	Cross-Ice Leads	X	X	X				
34.	Four-Blues Drop	X	X	X		X	X	
35.	Maine 2 on 0		X	X		X	X	
36.	Give and Go	X	X	X		X		
37.	Blues Bombs	X	X	X		X		
38.	Pivot Heaven		X	X		X	X	

Drill #	Drill	Fundamental	Timing	Speed	Conditioning	Transitions	Advanced skills	Fun
39.	2-on-0 Delay		X	X		X	X	
40.	Double Escape		X	X		X	X	
41.	Dartmouth Drill	X	X					
42.	St. John Pass and Shot	X	X	X				
43.	Double Give and Go	X	X	X				
44.	Quarterback	X	X					
45.	Dot Sprint	X	X	X				
46.	Revolver	X	X	X	X	X		
47.	High Octane		X	X	X		X	
48.	Indirect Break		X	X	X		X	
49.	Pass to Zones Transition		X	X		X	X	
50.	Pass Conditioner	X	X	X	X			
51.	One-Touch Warm-Up		X	X			X	X
52.	Tiger Shark	X	X	X	X	X		
53.	Ranger Drill		X	X		X	X	
54.	Finland One Touch		X	X	X	X	X	
55.	Cruise Control	X	X	X	X	X		
56.	Irish One Touch		X	X	X	X	X	X
57.	Swedish One Touch		X	X	X	X	X	X
58.	Team Canada One Time	X	X	X	X	X		
59.	Avalanche	X	X	X	X	X		
60.	Raider One Touch		X	X	X	X	X	X
61.	Erik's Loop	X	X	X	X			
62.	Kon Man's Delight	X	X	X		X		
63.	Doc's Give and Go		X	X	X	X	X	
64.	Orr's Transition Quickie	X	X	X		X		
65.	Mario's Regroup	X	X	X	X	X		
66.	Stretch Drill	X	X	X		X		
67.	Thunder Bay Stretch 2 on 0		X	X	X	X	X	X
68.	Timing 3 on 0	X	X	X	X	X		X
69.	Buccaneer 3 on 0	X	X	X	X	X		X
70.	Redhawk 4 on 0	X	X	X	X	X		X
71.	Long Leads	X	X	X	X	X		X
72.	Swing Daddy		X	X	X	X	X	X
73.	Continuous Traction 2 on 1		X	X	X	X	X	X
74.	One-Time Charlie		X	X	X	X	X	
75.	Tylenol 7		X	X	X	X	X	X

Foreword

Players and coaches who have studied and played hockey realize that this sport comprises many subtle skills beyond the obvious skating, scoring, and checking. Passing and receiving are also integral parts of the modern game, especially as they relate to transitional aspects of play, and are essential skills for players who desire to advance up the hockey developmental ladder.

Consider that during a typical National Hockey League game most players will touch and control the puck for a total of only 25 seconds. That's less than half of a minute during a 60-minute game! This means that for a majority of the time the puck is not controlled by individual players; instead, the puck is passed or received among participants. The puck is in a constant state of transition among individual players and between teams.

Whether players are attempting to advance the puck into an opponent's end or trying to exit their own defensive zone, passing and receiving are key aspects of play that must be understood and mastered if success is to follow. *Hockey Drills for Passing & Receiving* will help you understand and master these essential techniques and, as a result, become a better all-around player or coach.

Through practicing the many drills in the following pages, players will become polished and deadly passers while also becoming more proficient at receiving a pass, even under pressure-filled, gamelike situations. Coaches Gwozdecky and Stenlund provide an excellent guide for practicing passing and receiving that will translate into great goal-scoring opportunities during competition. And I, for one, am all for that!

Craig Hartsburg, Head Coach
Mighty Ducks of Anaheim

Acknowledgments

The authors express their gratitude to the following people for their assistance in the completion of this work: Carl Fama and the entire staff at the South Windsor Arena in Windsor, Ontario, for their assistance during the photo shoot; Jason Penner, Tony Williams, Tim Gleason, and Erik Stenlund, whose patience on the ice while the photos were taken was appreciated (hurry up to wait, eh guys); our photographer, Tom Roberts, a real pro who went above and beyond the call of duty during this assignment; Mark Hughes and the good folks at Easton Hockey, a quality company made up of quality people; Harold Konrad, for assisting with so many details; Paul O'Dacre, Bill Ferhman, and all the crew at Huron Hockey, you're simply the best; and last, but certainly not least, to Ted Miller, Cynthia McEntire, and all the other contributors to this book who work at Human Kinetics Publishing, thank you for making these projects so enjoyable and fulfilling.

Jason Penner, Tony Williams, Tim Gleason, and Erik Stenlund

Introduction

In September 1972 the former USSR sent a hockey team to North America to challenge the best players from the National Hockey League (NHL). The underdog Soviets were not expected to do well against an all-star team that included Phil Esposito, Bobby Clarke, and Paul Henderson. "The Summit Series" proved a vital learning experience for hockey experts around the world, however, as the Soviets surprised everyone by displaying tremendous skills. The NHL eventually came away with a narrow victory, but the very fabric of hockey changed forever. What was once considered a game of brute strength and force shifted course to focus on speed and skill. The Soviets left a lasting impression in many areas, none perhaps more so than in the realm of passing, receiving, and transition play.

This book continues the series of ice hockey skills and drill books being presented by the experts at Huron Hockey School. This information benefits both coaches and players attempting to move to the next level. The book provides practical suggestions for mastering passing and receiving, skills that the 1972 Soviet team demonstrated with great proficiency. Players who master the concepts presented here will learn to use passing and receiving as an integral part of both offensive and defensive hockey. Mastering these skills will put players in a position to control the flow of a game by controlling the key zones in which puck possession is vital.

The following drills will also help players improve game performance. The drills are designed to develop skills to apply directly to game situations. The benefits of this type of practice will be obvious immediately in competitive games—just as coaches at the Huron Hockey School have seen improvements in their players over the years of developing our methods of instruction.

Players and coaches can use this book for more productive individual and group practices. The activities are useful for virtually all levels of play and are beneficial for all groups—from beginners to experienced all-stars at the highest levels of the sport. This is, however, more than just another drill book. Also included are valuable tips and ideas for each activity to help players and coaches dramatically reduce the time required to master a given skill.

In collecting the drills, we started with simple activities that all players will find do-able, giving even beginning players a chance to succeed. We also provide methods for modifying the drills to challenge more experienced players. These modifications, or Drill Progressions, are often made by changing time and space parameters, which forces players to improve their skills. As their skill increases, players will be better able to perform at a faster pace in less space. Players will know they have improved because they will begin to see and feel the exciting results in practice and in games.

As you look at the drills, pay attention to the "Key Points" section of each activity. This section contains helpful ideas and suggestions for execution of the drills. Years of teaching and coaching experience have gone into developing these activities. The Key Points reflect the approaches of many coaches who have come through Huron Hockey, some of whom have reached the professional level. Their advice will guide players and coaches on the road to mastery and success.

Roller hockey enthusiasts can easily adapt many of the drills to a non-ice environment. Certain skills in ice hockey drilling patterns, however, may be affected in roller hockey by factors such as increased surface friction and different equipment. To incorporate some of the drills into roller hockey practice, try the drill first and modify it as necessary. Any problems will quickly become evident and adjustments may then be made.

How the Book Is Organized

The drills have been assembled with some specific objectives in mind. First, rather than combining drills from all phases of hockey, this book looks at one major aspect of play, namely, improving passing and receiving. This concept follows the organizational format of the other books in the series, which include *Hockey Drills for Puck Control*, *Hockey Drills for Scoring*, and *High-Performance Skating for Hockey*. This was done to avoid one of the pitfalls coaches and players encounter after purchasing a drill book or video or after attending a hockey seminar or clinic. Armed with a wealth of new information, many players and coaches return to practice filled with new ideas and ready to conquer the world! They inevitably realize, however, that many instructional materials are overly complicated and do not provide players with appropriate drills for their specific skill levels. Often the result is confusion and frustration for everyone. The books in this series do not attempt to provide drills for all situations—the game of hockey is far too complex. Instead, this book offers varied, flexible drills that incorporate other aspects of the game into passing and receiving activities. For an effective practice, coaches should emphasize the objectives for each session and drill so that players will clearly understand the intended objectives for that day.

Second, the drills in this book progress from simple activities at the beginning of each chapter to more difficult drills at the end. On a larger scale, each succeeding chapter of the book offers more challenging activities. This progression allows a wider range of players and coaches to find practical and useful information regardless of skill level.

Third, some chapters have specific drill sequences that build on a single concept. These sequences allow players to understand the objectives of the drills clearly and master the skills quickly. In chapters 4 and 5, for example, the "Wheel" and "Four Blues" patterns, respectively, are used as staple drills that are expanded in later drills. In addition, sample practice plans are included at the end of the book to guide coaches and players in integrating the drills into practices. To make planning easier, the Drill Finder at the front of the book identifies other aspects of play that are incorporated into specific drills.

This book makes little reference to shooting and scoring. Of course, the end goal in hockey is to score goals, and rarely is this objective accomplished without shooting (for a more detailed look at scoring, try *Hockey Drills for Scoring*, Human Kinetics, 1997). Because this book focuses on passing and receiving, however, aspects of how the drills relate to shooting are not discussed in great detail. For coaches and players wishing to integrate shooting into these drills, we suggest ways to modify individual drills to include a shot at the end of the activity.

Also, the drills rarely require extra equipment or substantial amounts of setup time. Most require only a stick, a puck, and some ice. As a result, they can be done with a minimum of wasted time and effort so you can spend valuable ice time doing the activities, not discussing them.

On a final note, you will notice that the skaters in the photos are not wearing helmets. The photo shoot was conducted under very controlled conditions during which there was no intense skating or physical contact between players. Human Kinetics and Huron Hockey, Inc. strongly advise players to always wear head and face protection during any practice or game situation.

We think you are going to enjoy the activities found in these pages while learning all you'll ever need to know about the finer aspects of passing and receiving. Now . . . let's get to work!

Key to Diagrams

X or O	Player/opposing player/pair of players
(C/L)	Coach or leader
D	Defenseman
F	Forward
R	Receiver
F^1 F^2	Designated forward
(G)	Goaltender
⟶	Forward skating
∿∿∿⟶	Forward skating with puck
⊂⊂⊂⊂	Backward skating
⊙⊙⊙⊙	Backward skating with puck
= or ‖	Stopping
	Turns
	Tight turns
⌢	Pivots (forward to backward, backward to forward)
------⟶	Passing
⟹	Shooting
⦂·	Pucks
△	Pylons or cones
	Hockey stick

Puck Exchange Principles

This chapter examines basic principles essential to improving passing and receiving skills. These principles represent the foundation of passing and receiving development. The drills in the following chapters assume that players understand these principles. Competence in this skill set is essential for players to develop the transition skills seen in modern hockey. As players progress, take time to reinforce the basic rules of passing and receiving; their skill advancement will be greatly enhanced. Some of the principles outlined here mirror important aspects of other skill areas including puck control and shooting. As with all skill development, practice is essential for success.

Principle #1: Find the Right Stick

The hockey stick is an often overlooked aspect of developing passing and receiving skills. With the technologies now available, type, size, and shape options have increased dramatically. Where once only wooden sticks were available, now players can choose from a variety of makes and models. When choosing a stick, players should consider their needs and style of play.

With all the options available, players should try as many different sticks as possible to find the right one. Over time, a player may develop a preference for one stick over another. A cheap and simple way to experiment with different sticks is to borrow a teammate's stick during practice. No absolute rules for selecting a hockey stick exist, but before choosing one, consider the following factors.

Stick Lie

To develop sound passing and receiving, it is important to have as much of the stick blade on the ice as possible. Stick lie affects this greatly. Stick lie is the angle formed by the shaft and the blade. The higher the lie number, the more upright the stick is when the blade is flat on the ice.

Lie numbers generally range from four to seven, although custom-made sticks may go as high as eight or nine. A player who skates slightly hunched at the waist in the style of Wayne Gretzky will require a four or five. Players who skate more upright need a higher lie number. A good way to check if a player is using a stick with the correct lie is to examine the bottom of the blade to ensure that it is wearing evenly, not just on the heel or toe (see figures 1.1 and 1.2).

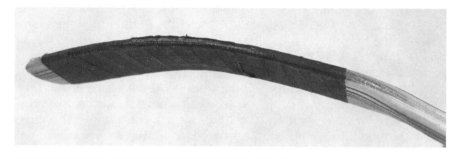

Figure 1.1 Even wear along the bottom of the stick blade

Figure 1.2 Uneven wear of the stick blade at the toe and at the heel

Stick Length

Stick length determines the puck position relative to the player's body and directly influences passing and receiving. A longer shaft forces the puck away from the body. Stick length can be important in executing or receiving a pass effectively, so it's important to try different lengths for both comfort and efficiency. The old adage that a stick should be cut at the same level as a player's nose or chin is not valid. Instead, players should experiment with different stick lengths to find the fit that feels most comfortable to them.

Blade Curvature

Younger players often mistakenly use a stick with more curvature than they are ready for, which can hinder their development of passing and receiving skills. Many choices exist in terms of curvature (see figure 1.3). For beginners, we recommend a blade with less curvature. Once sound foundational passing and receiving habits have been established, a player can switch to a blade with greater curvature. A sensible rule to follow is the younger the player, the straighter the blade.

Players should consider stick lie, stick length, and blade curvature before choosing a stick. Choosing the right stick requires the same amount of care as a baseball player takes in choosing a bat or a golfer takes in choosing golf clubs.

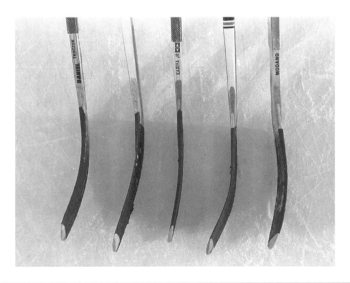

Figure 1.3 Blade curvature variations

Principle #2: Learn Proper Hand and Arm Positions

A player must understand the importance of proper hand, arm, and stick positions relative to the body to pass or receive a puck effectively. First, the player's hands should be a comfortable distance apart on the stick shaft. The further down the lower hand is placed, the more the player needs to bend at the waist. When passing a puck whether from the side or across the front of your body, your arms should be extended so that you can easily catch a glimpse of the puck on the blade while focusing on the intended target (see figure 1.4a). When receiving a pass, however, the stick blade should be held closer to the body (see figure 1.4b). It is easier to reach forward for a poor pass out in front than it is to pull the stick back on short notice. Holding the stick blade close to the body when receiving a pass also causes the player to focus the eyes more forward than down, an important point especially when cruising near a gigantic defenseman!

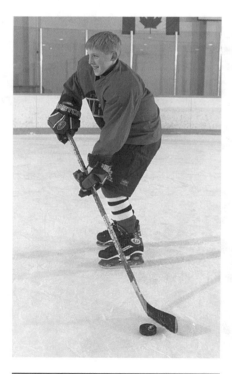 

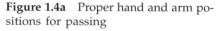

Figure 1.4a Proper hand and arm positions for passing

Figure 1.4b Proper hand and arm positions to receive a pass

Principle #3: Understand and Master the Three Zones

Mastering the three zones of passing and receiving is important whether using the forehand or backhand. The three zones are critical elements to success in passing and receiving. In passing, Zone 1 is the setup area at the beginning of the pass. Zone 2 is the release location, an extremely important element in delivering a smooth, effective pass. Zone 3 is the follow-through area into which the player carries the stick as the puck is released. Let's find these three zones in a passing sequence (see figure 1.5).

Notice the proper hand position and knee bend as the pass is initiated in Zone 1 (figure 1.5a). As the puck enters Zone 2, the passer prepares for release and must judge how long to keep the puck on the stick blade (figure 1.5b). Holding the puck too long results in the equivalent of a hook shot in golf; releasing too soon has the effect of a slice. Zone 2 is the critical zone for ensuring that the pass will be on target. In Zone 3, the player shifts the body weight toward the lead or front leg and points the stick blade at the intended target (figure 1.5c). The follow-through is also critical, much as in shooting, as

Figure 1.5a The puck begins behind the body in Zone 1

Figure 1.5b A sweeping motion carries the puck to the midline of the body through Zone 2

Figure 1.5c The passer follows through to the target and releases the puck in Zone 3

follow-through helps the player deliver the puck on target. All three zones must be practiced, first stationary and then in motion, to guarantee proper passing technique.

In addition, remember that these same three zones apply when you are passing from the side as opposed to across or in front of your body. With the side pass, the setup, or Zone 1, occurs behind the heels of the skates. Zone 2, or the release area, will happen near the toes of the skates. Zone 3, or the follow-through, occurs with the arms away from the body and the stick blade following through to the target.

Passing is only half of the equation. Most passes have someone waiting to receive them. Zones 1, 2, and 3 still apply in receiving, with some modification. In figure 1.6, notice how the player accepts the puck in front of the body, then draws it back through the remaining two zones.

The receiver must reach to accept the puck (see Zone 1; figure 1.6a), gain full control as the puck nears the midline of the body (see Zone 2; figure 1.6b), and then move the puck toward a buffer area to protect it and/or set up for a return pass (see Zone 3; figure 1.6c). We often tell players to treat a passed puck as if it were an egg, using soft, relaxed hands to gain immediate control, especially of a hard pass. Understanding the three zones in passing and receiving is a critical step in developing mastery.

Figure 1.6a The receiver reaches for the puck in Zone 1. In this example, the player receives the pass on the backhand

Figure 1.6b The puck approaches the midline of the body in Zone 2

Figure 1.6c The receiver buffers the puck, preparing for a setup or return pass in Zone 3

Principle #4: Sweep the Puck— Don't Slap It!

The purpose of passing in any sport is to allow the target to receive the pass successfully. It would make no sense for John Elway to throw a football pass as hard as he can to a target 10 feet away. Similarly, why throw a hard-to-catch, wounded-duck pass rather than a perfect spiral? In hockey, slapping the puck leads to unusual outcomes. The puck might dance along the ice so that no receiver could possibly control it. Or, the passing speed generated by slapping the puck may not give a teammate time to set up for a clean reception. As described earlier, moving smoothly through the three zones of passing is the most effective way to deliver the puck. Avoid slapping while passing to improve both control and accuracy.

Principle #5: Players Away From the Puck Must Read Proper Positioning

The receiver helps create a successful passer when the receiver is in position to receive the puck. Players without the puck make a passer's job easier by moving into open ice, entering the passer's line of sight and creating an open passing lane (see figure 1.7ab). Without this play away from the puck, even the most skilled passer fights an uphill battle. Players without the puck should never just skate around and expect a pass. These players must move into open areas to become a legitimate candidate to receive the puck from a teammate.

Attention to detail separates excellent from average passers. Along with the preceding principles, players should remember the following points to improve passing and receiving.

Figure 1.7a The player behind the opponent cannot be seen and is not open to receive a pass

Figure 1.7b   The player moves to open ice to become a target option

When passing . . .

- The first passing option is always tape to tape (the puck leaves the passer's stick and goes directly to the receiver's stick). The phrase *tape to tape* refers to the puck touching the black tape used on a hockey stick blade. Tape to tape is the fastest, most efficient way to move the puck.
- If tape to tape is not possible, pass to a zone or area to which a teammate can skate. The principle of "taking something off" the fastball in baseball also applies to passing in hockey. A passer might slow the speed of the pass, take something off it, to locate the puck so that a teammate will be able to retrieve it easily.
- Avoid passing into the skates or behind the body of the receiver. Receivers of such passes are forced to look down or reach behind themselves. Both scenarios are dangerous in leagues that allow contact. Passing the puck slightly ahead of the target allows the receiver to keep the eyes forward, not down, reducing unwanted contact with opponents.

When receiving . . .

- Position the stick blade on the ice for easy retrieval. If the player holds the stick at waist level or higher during skating, it will take time to bring the blade into contact with the ice surface. The extra time needed may result in a missed pass, all because the receiver was not in a position to receive the puck.
- Use the stick blade as a target for the passer. The simple act of providing a visual cue for the passer will help improve passing efficiency.
- Call for the puck! Teammates should not assume that the passer sees them and will deliver a perfect pass. Alerting the passer improves the chances of a pass being delivered. Calling for the puck is one of the most overlooked yet vital aspects of effective receiving.

Practice both forehand and backhand passing and receiving. Don't cheat by switching the puck to the forehand! Forehand play might be easier and more comfortable, especially early in a player's career, but the time will come when the player will have to execute passes from both sides. In games, players usually do not have time to move the puck from back to front. Start practicing backhand passing and receiving as early as possible to reap the rewards for years to come.

Now let's put these basic principles and details to work. The next chapter introduces fundamental passing and receiving activities and drills.

Evaluation and Development of Fundamentals

Coaches can use these foundational drills to introduce or review passing and receiving skills and assess or test players' skill levels. Players can use the drills to test accuracy and quickness in executing passing and receiving skills in a noncontact environment. The key is to find the use that best fits your goals and needs.

Adapt these drills for half-ice situations or lane drilling depending on practice circumstances. Because coaches and players often have restricted ice space, many of the drills are adaptable.

It is important to understand two key aspects for drilling at this elementary level. First, some of these activities are stationary, a logical starting point for developing the necessary hand-eye skills needed to improve passing and receiving. A player who cannot perform a skill while stationary probably cannot do it in motion! As confidence and comfort develop, progress into passing and receiving while in motion.

Second, to maximize each player's repetitions, use a wave formation whether in a full-ice or half-ice format. Wave formations maximize available ice time and allow coaches to identify potential problems for specific players immediately. Problems will be seen easily, since the action occurs directly in front of the coach.

To ensure proper progress, keep in mind the principles discussed in chapter 1. Simplify activities that seem too difficult so players can achieve a measure of success. As skill increases and the drills become easier, move on to more challenging ones. It makes no sense to practice drills that are either too simple or too demanding, as either extreme may frustrate both players and coaches.

The following drills can be used at almost any level and are presented progressively from simple to more difficult. Use the included guidelines to make drills more challenging for advanced players. Resist the temptation to skip ahead to more difficult drills; master the basic drills first to develop well-rounded skills. Even professionals practice the basics!

① Hit the Cone

Purpose

- Introduce or review basic passing and receiving principles
- Assess passing and receiving skill levels

Equipment   One cone or pylon for each player; three to four pucks per player

Time   Two to three minutes, depending on skill level

Procedure

1. Players are located around the boards with a supply of three or four pucks each and one cone or pylon each.
2. The cone is placed against the boards. Players begin at a close distance, 5 to 10 feet from the cone. Players attempt to pass the puck so that it hits the cone.
3. Once all pucks are passed, players retrieve them and try another round of passes, keeping score of how many times they hit the cone successfully.

Key Points

- Players should use the three zones for both passing and receiving while shifting their weight from the back to the front leg during the passing or receiving motion.
- Practice all of the principles of passing and receiving, especially hand and arm location.

Drill Progressions

- Players should move further away from the pylon to test long-distance accuracy. Or, they should replace the pylon with another puck to reduce the size of the target (see diagram).
- Have a contest to see who can hit the cone or puck the most times (total count) or who can hit the cone or puck the most times consecutively.

Hit the Cone

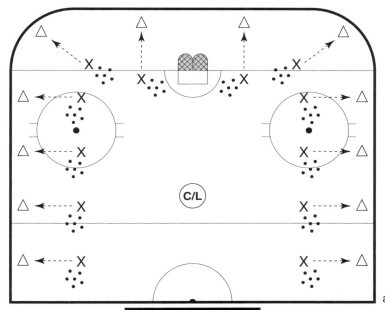

a

Drill Progression

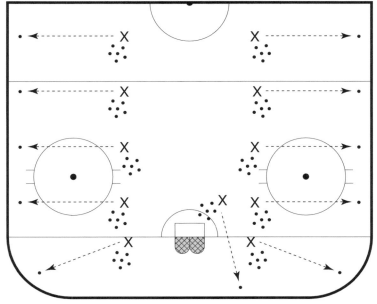

b

② Stationary Passing and Receiving

Purpose

- Introduce or review basic passing and receiving principles
- Assess passing and receiving skill levels

Equipment One puck per pair of players

Time Two to three minutes, depending on skill level

Procedure

1. Players assemble in two equal lines facing one of the goal lines.
2. With the two lines of players approximately 10 feet apart, the leader (coach or player) partners each player with another player from the opposite line.
3. Players attempt stationary passes to their partners, either forehand or backhand depending on the direction they are facing. After three to five minutes, players turn and face the opposite goal line, forcing them to use the other passing motion (either forehand or backhand). Continue the drill for another three to five minutes.

Key Points

- Players should use the three zones for both passing and receiving while shifting their weight from the back to the front leg during the passing or receiving motion.
- Practice all of the principles of passing and receiving, especially hand and arm location.

Drill Progressions

- Players should move further apart to test long-distance accuracy (see diagram).
- Advanced players might attempt a "saucer" pass.

Stationary Passing and Receiving

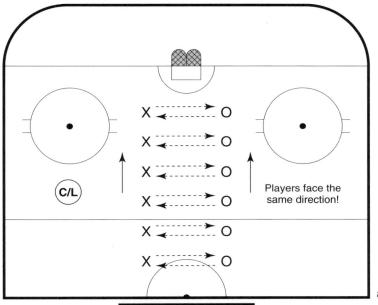

Players face the same direction!

a

Drill Progression

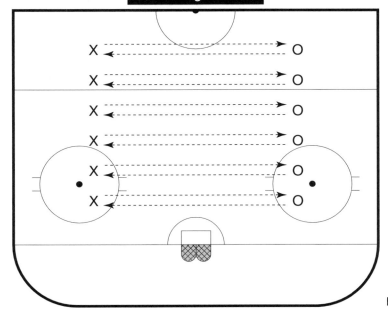

b

③ Intercept

Purpose

- Introduce fundamental passing and receiving mechanics in a stationary drill

Equipment   One puck per player

Time   Two to four minutes

Procedure

1. Players work in pairs, standing 10 to 15 feet apart and facing each other. Both players have a puck on their stick blade.
2. The first player says, "go," and passes a puck toward the partner's stick blade. The second player then releases a pass with the intention of hitting or intercepting the other puck.
3. After several attempts are made on the forehand, players attempt the same activity using backhand passes.

Key Points

- Watch for "lazy arms" (hands and arms too close to the body).
- Wait until the first puck is on course before the second partner attempts to intercept.
- Timing of the second player is key for this drill.

Drill Progressions

- Have groups of three or four players practice together, with one player passing first and the other passers attempting to intercept (see diagram).

Intercept 3

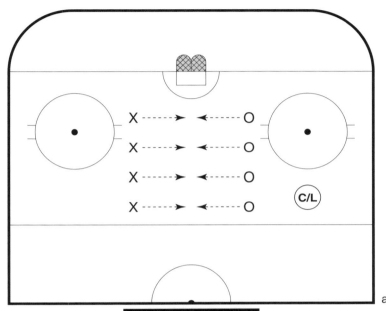

a

Drill Progression

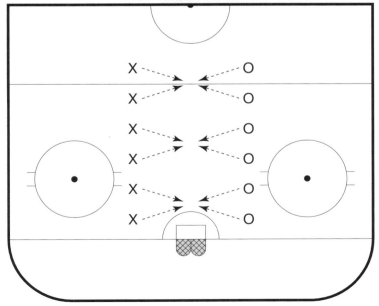

b

④ Pepper

Purpose

- Introduce basic passing and receiving skills and identify player skill levels

Equipment One puck per player

Time 2-4 minutes, 30-second sets, 5 sets maximum

Procedure

1. Groups of four or five players stand around the rink in a semicircle approximately 12–15 feet across.
2. One player, the designated receiver, receives and passes back to every member of the group during the 30-second set.
3. The receiver may pivot the feet to face another passer. The receiver cannot move, however, from a designated space.
4. The designated receiver passes and receives the puck with alternate group members for 30 seconds, then rotates with another player who becomes the new designated receiver.

Key Points

- Check that players have (a) the proper hand location on the stick, (b) the arms away from the hips, (c) the entire blade of the stick on the ice, (d) the knees bent, and (e) the feet stationary.
- Coaches can circulate to assist players where needed.

Drill Progressions

- Increase the speed of each receiving action, perhaps attempting a one-time pass or reception if skill level warrants. Have the receiver and others call for the puck each time it is passed. Add a second puck.
- Have three players form a stationary line with the center player as the receiver. Alternate passing back and forth with the two wingers, switching between forehand and backhand (see diagram).

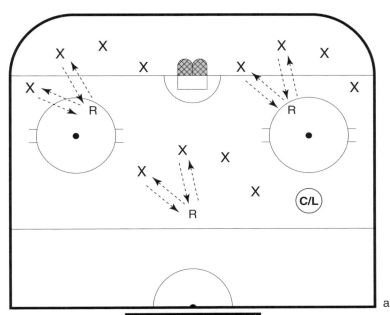

a

Drill Progression

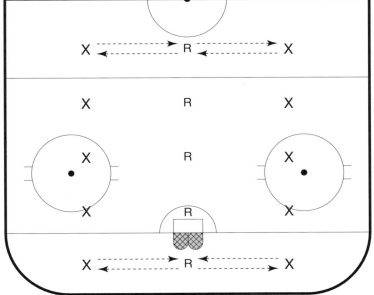

b

(5) Self-Serve

Purpose

- Reinforce proper forehand and backhand passing technique while introducing motion into the skill set

Equipment Four to 10 pylons, one puck per player

Time Three to five minutes, depending on skill level

Procedure

1. Players are located in equal groups at either end of the ice surface, in alternate corners.
2. Four to 10 pylons are spaced evenly along both sides of the ice, approximately five feet from the boards.
3. When the coach blows the whistle, one player from each line skates forward, passes the puck off the boards between the pylons, and retrieves the pass.
4. Once the player passes all the pylons, the player moves to the back of the line at the other end of the rink.

Key Points

- Players should keep feet and hands moving at the same time.
- Once everyone has completed the route, groups switch corners so that they must practice passing from the other side of their stick blades.
- The distance between pylons is determined by skill level—the lower the skills, the fewer the pylons.

Drill Progressions

- Try to move faster through the drill.
- Increase the number of pylons, thereby increasing the number of passes.

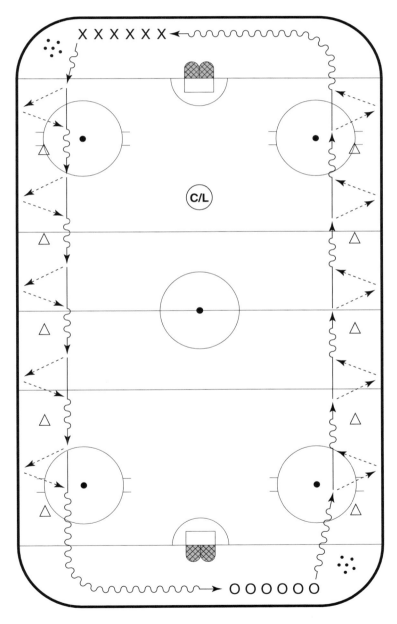

6 Passing Relay

Purpose

- Reinforce proper forehand and backhand passing

Equipment   One puck for each group of three players

Time   Three to five minutes

Procedure

1. Players work in groups of three, with two stationary players located near one sideboard and a single player located across the ice near the opposite sideboard.
2. The player with the puck skates forward halfway across the ice and passes to the waiting player on the opposite sideboard; the first player then assumes the position of the player who received the pass.
3. The receiving player carries the puck back across the ice, passing to the last player in the threesome.
4. The drill continues across the ice.

Key Points

- Players are forced to use both forehand and backhand techniques to pass and receive.
- The Passing Relay is not a race. Instead, players are asked to make perfect passes while attempting to receive passes cleanly.

Drill Progressions

- Increase the speed of repetitions, or make a minimum amount of reps a requirement for a specific length of time.
- Have players receive a pass then pivot backward and skate with the puck (see diagram).

Passing Relay

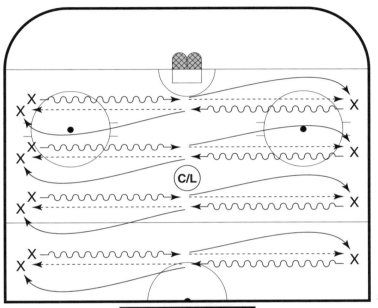

a

Drill Progression

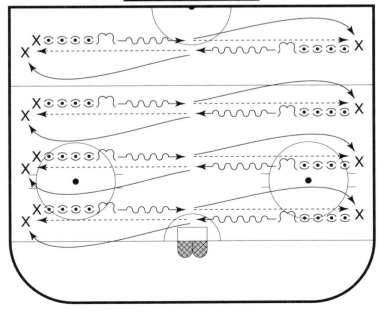

b

7 Box Pass

Purpose

- Encourage proper passing and receiving through a group activity

Equipment One puck for each group of four players

Time Two to four minutes

Procedure

1. Players in groups of four assume stationary positions in a box or square format anywhere on the ice.
2. Passes between players are made in a clockwise direction using either forehand or backhand motion.
3. After one minute, players pass in a counterclockwise fashion, and they must use the other side of their stick blades.

Key Points

- Emphasize keeping the hands away from the body and all other proper passing mechanics.
- Remind players that this is not a race. The box pass is a drill to work on perfect passing.
- Make sure that both forehand and backhand passing are attempted.

Drill Progressions

- Move from a slow to a faster activity.
- Try two pucks moving at once.
- Players can pass then follow their pass, turning the drill into a passing and skating activity (see diagram).

Box Pass

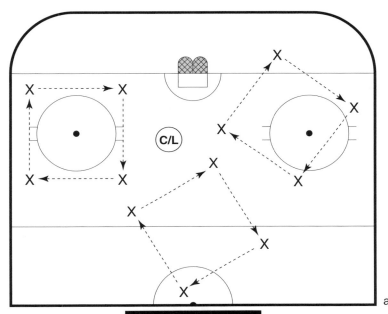

a

Drill Progression

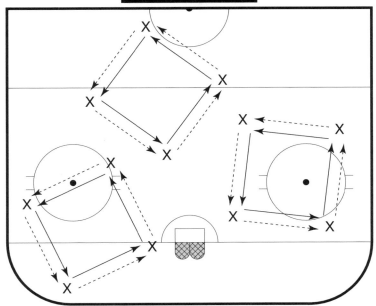

b

27

8 Escalator

Purpose

- Reinforce forward passing and skating
- Introduce passing and receiving at various distances

Equipment   One puck for each pair of players

Time   Three to five minutes, depending on group size and skill level

Procedure

1. Players work in two equal groups, positioned approximately 10 feet apart near the goal area.
2. Players skate forward in pairs, passing a puck between them until they reach the far goal area.
3. Then they skate to opposite sides of the goal line and begin skating back to the end where they began the drill.
4. Players continue passing long range across the full width of the ice until they return to the line. Switch lines for the next attempt.

Key Points

- Once a pair reaches the near blue line, the next pair can begin.
- If using only half the ice rink, turn at the center red line and head back.
- By switching lines, players use both forehand and backhand passes.

Drill Progressions

- Increase the speed of the drill.
- Designate a minimum number of passes to be made.
- Add pivoting and backward skating components to a portion of the drill.

Escalator

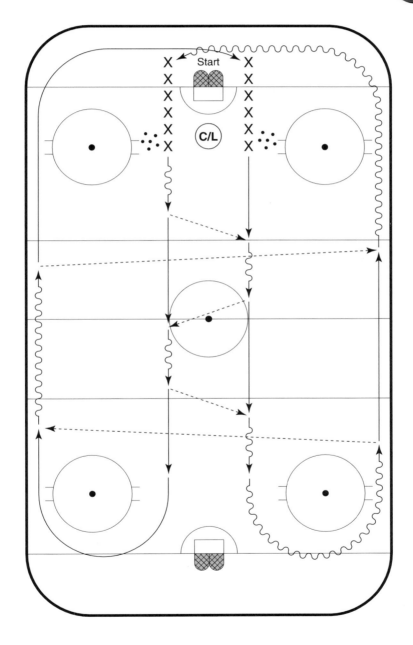

⑨ Full-Ice Reverse

Purpose

- Work on passing and receiving skills, skating, and timing

Equipment   One puck per each pair of players

Time   Four to five minutes

Procedure

1. The Full-Ice Reverse is similar to the Escalator drill, except this time the two groups of players are located in one corner of the rink.
2. Pairs are positioned 10 feet apart and pass the puck the distance of the ice.
3. At the far end, players skate around the net and switch sides, continuing to pass until they reach the opposite corner from where they began the drill.
4. Once all players have finished, the drill is run again in the opposite direction, moving players through both forehand and backhand passing.

Key Points

- This drill is not a race. Emphasize sound technique and timing.
- Once a pair reaches the near blue line, the next pair may begin.
- Watch for proper mechanics as noted in the opening chapter.

Drill Progressions

- Have players attempt a pivot and skate backward after skating past the net at the far end.
- Increase speed and number of reps.
- Try using two pucks.

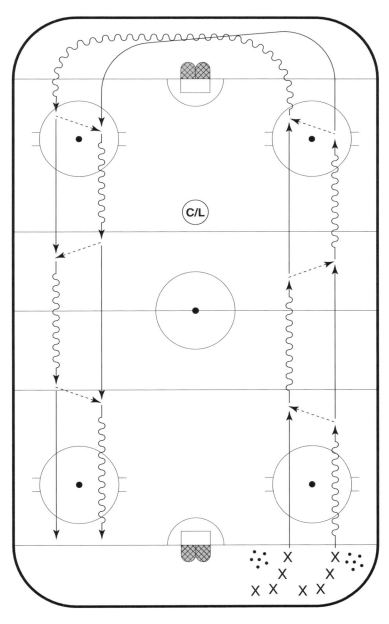

10 The Weave

Purpose

- Develop passing and receiving skills while practicing timing

Equipment   One puck per pair of players

Time   Three to five minutes

Procedure

1. The Weave uses a similar path as in the Full-Ice Reverse drill, with two lines of players set up in a single corner.
2. The player with the puck skates forward and passes to his or her partner. The passer then follows the pass, skating hard to cut in behind the receiver.
3. The receiver slides toward the other side so that both players switch their positions.
4. This pattern continues around the far net and finishes in the opposite corner from where the drill began.

Key Points

- Players must remember to accelerate after they pass to catch up to their partners as they switch positions.
- Timing is key, so one player cannot get too far ahead of his or her partner.
- The receiver can help tremendously by sliding across once the pass is received.

Drill Progressions

- Demand higher speed throughout the route skated.
- Try the same drill skating backward.
- Have more advanced players attempt to exchange two pucks during the drill.

The Weave

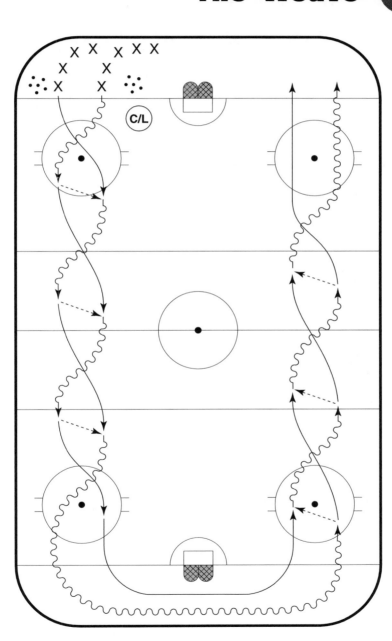

3 Focused Warm-Up Drills

Are you among the growing number of players who consider warm-ups to be boring and a waste of time? Are you a coach trying to warm up players and conduct a full practice with limited ice time? Take heart: the activities in this chapter will put some sizzle into this important phase of practice. Passing and receiving skills are natural for warm-up drills and get the heart pumping and the muscles loosened for the hard work to come. Don't look at warming up as drudgery. Instead, see the warm-up as a chance to prepare for practice while working on a skill set at the same time.

In hockey, as with any sport, the warm-up is important for many reasons. It is generally acknowledged that including some form of warm-up in your practice decreases the likelihood of nagging injuries, such as muscle pulls, which might otherwise occur if the body is not prepared properly for on-ice performance. In addition, warming up and stretching increase players' flexibility, which can be important when confronting the physically demanding challenges that occur during a game or practice.

It is especially important to introduce young players to warm-up drills. Although six- or seven-year-olds rarely pull leg or stomach muscles as a result of playing hockey, the positive implications of warming up these young players go far beyond any immediate benefits. Stressing the need to warm up early in young athletes' careers establishes a routine that will become more and more important as their bodies mature. Flexibility decreases over time, and a proper warm-up will be essential as young athletes continue their careers. Ask any adult weekend warrior whether a warm-up is necessary to appreciate the need for instilling these work habits early.

For our purposes, the warm-up phase of practice should serve two specific goals. First, players use this time to increase their core body temperatures in preparation for the more demanding workout to follow.

This type of thorough warm-up is often referred to as a *physiological warm-up* and can take up to 20 minutes. Unfortunately for many coaches and players, that 20 minutes might represent a significant portion of allotted ice time, making an extended warm-up difficult to achieve. If time is a factor, especially with younger age groups where the risk of injury due to reduced warm-up time is relatively low, the coach might opt for what is commonly referred to as a *sport-* or *skill-specific warm-up*. These activities take three to five minutes on the ice and include drills that specifically relate to the overall objectives for that particular practice. This practical warm-up will serve as the basis for the majority of drills in this chapter.

As an example of a skill-specific warm-up, let's assume that a coach wants to emphasize passing and receiving skills with a specific focus on backhand passing. The warm-up might include two or three quick activities that begin or end with some type of backhand pass either to a partner or along the sideboards. Players will begin to realize what the focus area or main objectives are for that day's practice. Coaches then can discuss and explain the objectives with the players before beginning the focused practice. While executing the drills, the players

will discover plenty of room for personal improvement in the specific skill area on which they are working.

Use the following drills as warm-up activities, or alter the intensity or difficulty to suit other specific applications. Remember, warm-up is the time to begin building momentum and intensity for the rest of practice. The drills you choose for the warm-up should reflect this intended progression. Do not expect players to execute high-intensity drills the moment they step on the ice, even if they have stretched before practice.

Alternate Passing and Receiving

Purpose

- Reinforce proper forehand and backhand passing

Equipment   One puck per pair of players

Time   Two to three minutes

Procedure

1. Partners are in stationary positions 5 to 10 feet apart anywhere on the ice.
2. Players alternate passing and receiving forehand and backhand targets, with the passer attempting to make perfect passes to the receiver's stick blade.
3. Each time the puck is received, the passer pivots to the opposite position, either forehand or backhand.
4. Players continue to pass and alternate sides until the whistle is blown.

Key Points

- Players are forced to execute both forehand and backhand passes and receptions.
- This drill is not a race. Players should focus on making sound, sweeping motions while passing and learn to receive the puck cleanly.

Drill Progressions

- Increase the speed of repetitions, and set a minimum number of passes during a set time.
- Partners can move further apart, increasing the length of passes.

Alternate Passing and Receiving

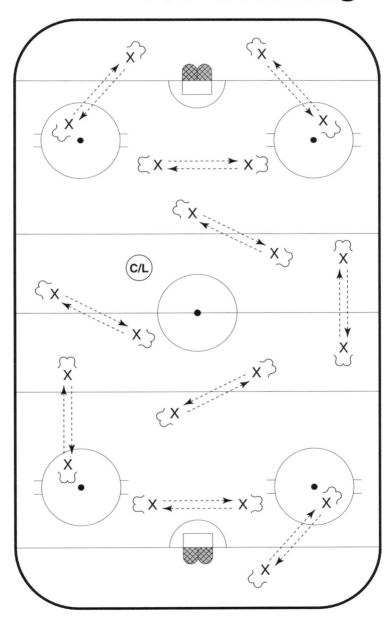

11

12 Stop-and-Go Passing and Receiving

Purpose

- Provide a warm-up activity that requires proper technique and thinking

Equipment   One puck per each pair of players

Time   Four to five minutes

Procedure

1. Players are paired with a single puck and begin in one corner of the rink.
2. The receiver skates forward, and the passer sends the puck to the receiver.
3. After accepting the pass, the receiver stops and waits for the passer to skate forward before returning the pass.
4. Players must skate immediately after passing. The drill continues around the rink to be completed in the opposite corner from where it began.

Key Points

- This can be a very challenging drill. The stop-and-go nature forces players to think about their responsibilities with or without the puck.
- The stationary passer must remember to set up for good mechanics after each stop. Passers should keep the hands away from the sides of the body.

Drill Progressions

- Increase speed.
- Attempt the drill while skating backward.
- Alternate forward and backward skating with each pass reception.
- Use this drill in a sequence with drills #9 and #10.

Stop-and-Go Passing and Receiving

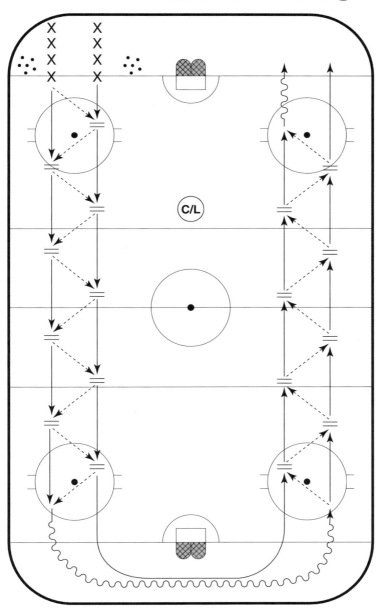

12

13) Swing Warm-Up

Purpose

- Practice in-close passing and receiving
- Introduce the concepts of transition in a beginning drill

Equipment   A cache of pucks for each group

Time   Three to four minutes

Procedure

1. Players begin in four equal groups located at the offside face-off dots (the neutral zone).
2. One player passes to the first player in the opposite group, skates beyond the center red line, and then turns toward the end from which he or she started.
3. The pass is returned, and the player goes in for a shot on goal.
4. The first receiver pulls a puck from the cache to initiate the next pass. The drill runs toward the opposite end of the ice.

Key Points

- The Swing Warm-Up is also a great drill to reinforce the importance of pivoting while turning so that the players never turn their backs to the puck.
- Remind passers never to put the puck behind the receiver; instead, they should lead far in front of the receiver if necessary so the receiver can skate after the loose puck.

Drill Progressions

- Have players execute both forehand and backhand passes.
- Add a second player from the group across the ice and make the shot on goal a 2 on 0 or a 1 on 1.

Swing Warm-Up

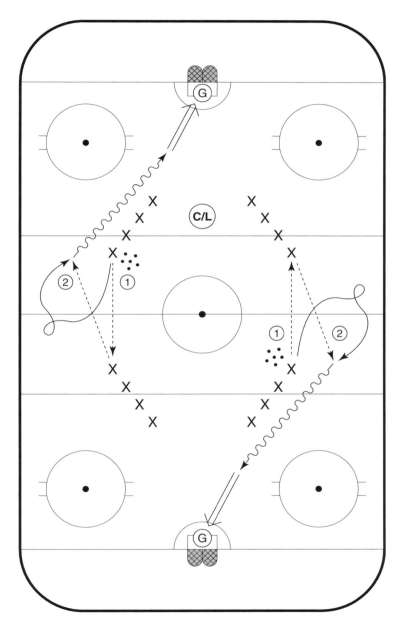

Monkey in the Middle Progression

Purpose

- Allow players to experiment with different types of passing through a fun warm-up

Equipment   First stage: one puck per group; second and third stages: two pucks per group

Time   Four to five minutes

Procedure

1. Players in groups of five or six stand around any face-off circle. One player (the monkey) stands in the middle; the outside players remain stationary until the third stage of the drill.
2. First stage: Players perform stop-and-go passing with the monkey (the player in the middle) trying to intercept any passes.
3. Second stage: Two pucks are used at the same time with two monkeys in the middle.
4. Third stage: The players around the circle may move but cannot pass to a player directly beside them.

Key Points

- Most young athletes will remember this activity from their physical education classes.
- The circle players should remain stationary until the third stage.
- Because they are not allowed to pass to anyone beside them, players must attempt to thread the needle through an oncoming monkey, thereby increasing passing accuracy.

Drill Progressions

- Have players practice a couple of sets using backhand passes only.
- To add conditioning, have players do three quick push-ups or sit-ups after each pass they make.

Monkey in the Middle Progression

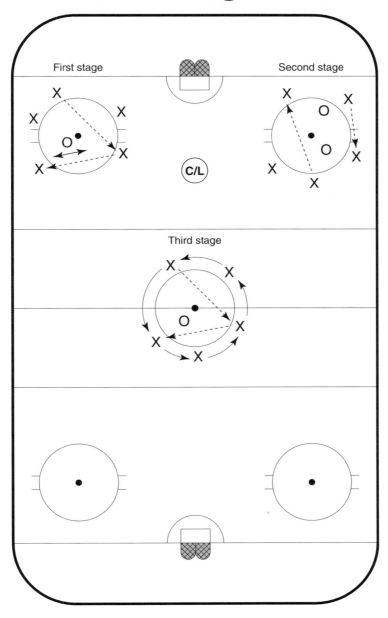

First stage

Second stage

C/L

Third stage

15 Drexie Warm-Up

Purpose

- Practice receiving and staying onside at an opponent's blue line

Equipment   A cache of pucks in the center circle

Time   Three to four minutes

Procedure

1. Players begin in equal groups in all four corners (two equal groups if using a half-ice format for practice).
2. The coach or leader stands next to the pucks in the center circle. Alternating players from either corner skate toward the coach past the blue line and loop back along the boards.
3. The coach passes a puck, and the player receives it while staying onside, finishing the drill with a shot on goal. The player then switches to another group to try the drill from the opposite side.

Key Points

- Players must turn to both their strong and weak sides, helping skating skills as well as receiving skills.
- Players should remember to keep the stick on the ice for an easy, quick reception.
- This is another good drill for practicing pivoting toward the puck carrier, rather than turning the back to the play!

Drill Progressions

- Add a chaser to increase speed.
- Turn into a 2 on 0 by having both sides go at the same time.

Drexie Warm-Up

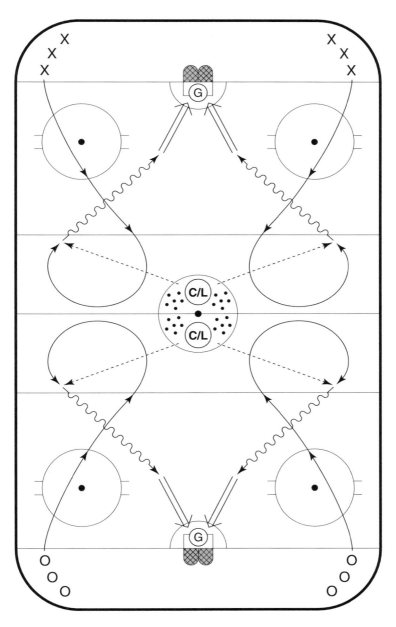

16 Mason Partner Pass

Purpose

- Practice passing and receiving in a warm-up while skating both forward and backward

Equipment One puck per pair of players

Time Three to four minutes

Procedure

1. Players begin in pairs at one corner of the rink.
2. One player skates forward while the other skates backward the entire length of the ice, exchanging the puck as they go.
3. Once they round the net at the far end, the players reverse roles and complete the drill to the opposite corner from where they began.

Key Points

- The Mason Partner Pass forces players to pass and receive while skating backward.
- Players should remember to have the stick blade close to the ice at all times.

Drill Progressions

- Once the skill level is raised, attempt to use one-touch passes only.
- Attempt to alternate passes off the boards to make the drill more challenging.
- Increase the tempo to increase the difficulty.

Mason Partner Pass

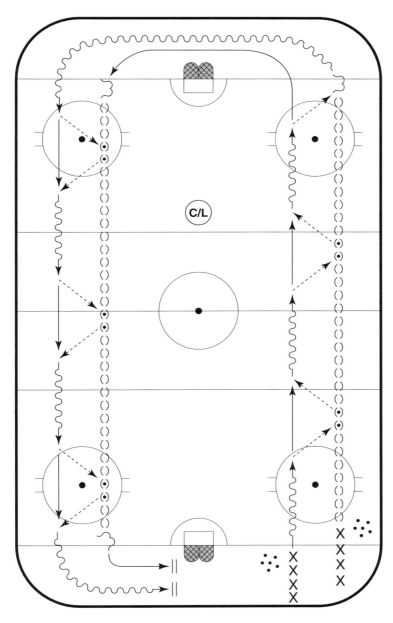

Six-Line Wave Progression

Purpose

- Practice passing and receiving using a wave formation

Equipment   One puck per pair of players

Time   Four to five minutes

Procedure

1. Players are in six lines situated along the boards at one end of the rink. For the first part of the drill, lines 1 and 2 work together, lines 3 and 4 work together, and lines 5 and 6 work together.
2. On the whistle, the first players from each line skate toward the other end of the rink, passing and receiving as directed by the coach. With each whistle, a new group of six players leaves, each player skating with his or her partner from the next line.
3. At the coach's direction, three lines join together (lines 1, 2, and 3 and lines 4, 5, and 6) to make it a three-player passing activity. The coach decides what types of passes are to be used for each successive wave.

Key Points

- This drill is a great way to use both ice space and players positively. Coaches can have players attempt a variety of passing and receiving maneuvers using the wave formation.
- Timing is important. Players should not to get too far ahead of their partners or linemates for any given drill.

Drill Progressions

- Try this with players skating backward, or include a three-player weave as a finishing activity (see diagram).

Six-Line Wave Progression

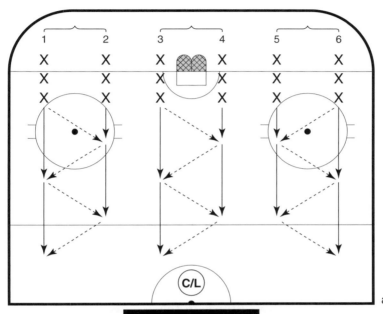

a

Drill Progression

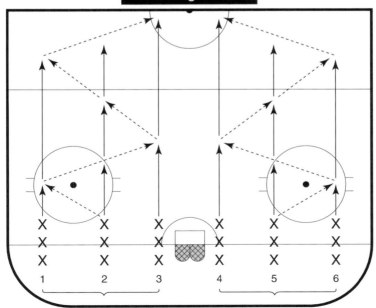

b

18 Back and Forth

Purpose

- Develop foot and hand speed and foot, hand, and eye coordination

Equipment Two pylons and one puck per pair of players

Time Three to four minutes

Procedure

1. Players are paired, one passer and one receiver, with roles reversed halfway through the drill.
2. Two pylons are placed 5 feet apart. The passer is stationary about 10 feet behind the middle of the pylon opening.
3. The receiver skates forward through the middle of the pylons and pivots to skate backward while moving around the outside of one pylon. The passer can pass the puck anytime while the receiver skates.
4. The drill continues with the receiver skating a pattern as seen in the diagram. Halfway through the activity, the coach blows a whistle and the players switch roles.

Key Points

- The Back and Forth drill is an excellent way to work on passing and receiving while improving pivoting.
- Both players must be ready (stick blades on the ice) as either player may pass whenever he or she chooses.

Drill Progressions

- Try the drill beginning with backward skating through the middle of the two pylons (see diagram).
- Put two pairs together. Have the four players do the activity using a single puck.

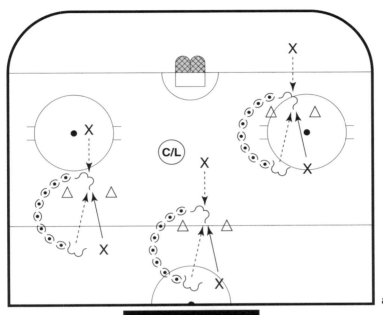

a

Drill Progression

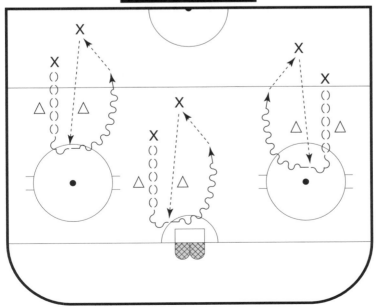

b

⟨19⟩ Stagger Passing and Receiving

Purpose

- Provide multiple passing and receiving opportunities in a warm-up activity

Equipment   One puck for each player except for the designated receivers

Time   Two to three minutes

Procedure

1. The coach designates two, three, or four receivers for each group (depending on skill level) who will be situated between the two blue lines in the neutral zone.
2. All other players are in two equal groups located catty-corner at opposite ends of the rink.
3. On the whistle, the first player from each group skates out and passes to a stationary receiver in the neutral zone, making sure to keep in motion the whole time.
4. The receiver returns the puck to the passer who then passes it to the next receiver.
5. After passing to all the receivers, the passer shoots on goal at the far end to complete the drill, then skates to the back of the opposite line.

Key Points

- The more receivers in the neutral zone, the tougher the drill.
- Emphasize accuracy, not speed, when first attempting this drill.

Drill Progressions

- Increase the intensity and speed of the activity.
- Have the first receiver in the neutral zone go to the back of the line, and all other receivers rotate one spot with successive passes. The shooter assumes the last receiving position in the sequence, so he or she must be alert after taking a shot.

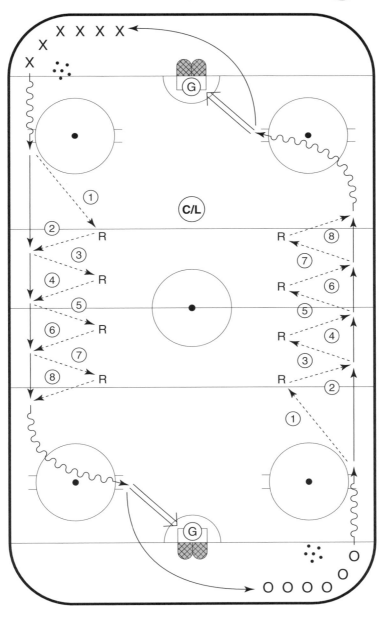

⟨20⟩ Leamington Warm-Up

Purpose

- Provide a high-tempo warm-up that develops skating, passing and receiving, and timing

Equipment   Two pylons

Time   Four to five minutes

Procedure

1. Forwards stand in opposite corners; defensemen are split equally into two groups positioned along the sideboards in the neutral zone.
2. Play begins when forward 1 (F^1) and forward 2 (F^2) leave at the same time around the top of the circle. F^1 passes to F^2 who shoots. Both forwards loop around their respective face-off circles. F^2 picks up a second puck and passes to F^1 who shoots. The forwards stay in front of the net.
3. In the neutral zone, one defenseman weaves between the two pylons as shown, always facing the end zone while skating, which requires pivoting. Near each pylon, one of the other defensemen passes a puck to the skating defenseman who returns it.
4. After the forwards have shot, the defenseman skates up the middle and shoots a puck on goal.

Key Points

- The defenseman who is shooting must wait for both forwards to shoot before proceeding toward the net; therefore, timing is important here.
- Forwards should screen, deflect, and look for rebounds.

Drill Progressions

- We think this is about all that is needed out of one drill!

Leamington Warm-Up

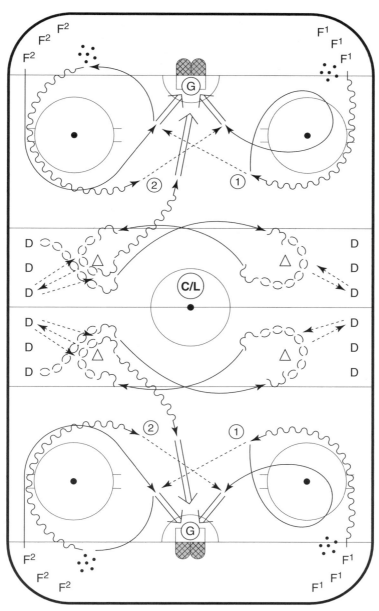

Puck Exchanges Through the Wheel

One of the legacies of the great Russian teams of the 1970s and 1980s was their tremendous skill in passing and receiving even at high speeds, while being attacked, or under pressure. Those skills can be seen today in the Russian stars who have emigrated to the National Hockey League. Oleg Tverdovsky, Sergei Fedorov, Igor Larionov, and other great Russian skaters possess the highest passing and receiving skills perhaps ever seen in professional hockey. This skill set can be traced back to a classic Russian drilling pattern the earlier Soviet teams practiced every day. Known by many as the "Russian Wheel" or "Soviet Circle," this dynamic way to practice both passing and receiving is the focus of this chapter.

In its simplest form, the Russian Wheel uses the center ice faceoff circle as a road map for an entire series of drills that focus on a number of skill sets including passing and receiving. The center circle area is used to introduce a variety of passing and receiving sequences, from a basic single-pass pattern to more complex passing and receiving drills. Virtually any aspect of specialized skill or team play can be initiated through this basic activity. These different combinations are laid out through the drill sequences in this chapter.

The Russian Wheel is still a viable drill option in practice situations where full ice is not available; coaches and players will just need to make some easy modifications. Players use the width of their side of the ice to simulate a circle, with pylons marking the outer edges of an imaginary circle. Ideally, two nets are used across either side of the end zone. If only one net is available, however, a "goal" can be constructed using pylons as goal posts. A half-ice practice situation should not have any impact on the effectiveness of these drills if the objectives and flow for this set of drill patterns are explained to the players completely.

Principles of Offensive Attack

The Wheel provides a good opportunity to introduce players to key principles of offensive attack off a pass. The Wheel can simulate breakouts or transitions leading to offensive attack opportunities. The practice of breaking through the Soviet Circle and completing a rush helps create successful offensive opportunities during a game. As players practice the Wheel, remind them of these important points:

• *Always give up the puck to an open teammate who is further up the ice!* Effective passing allows a team to gain zones and advance into an opponent's territory quickly and decisively. Using passing to advance the puck up the ice benefits a team in two ways: first, the team improves its chances of scoring a goal simply by being closer to

the opponent's net; and, second, the old adage of "the best defense is a good offense" comes into effect. Moving the puck forward increases the team's offensive abilities and restricts possible chances of scoring against the team's own goaltender.

• *Never go offside when outnumbering the opponent at their blue line.* Don't waste good offensive opportunities by going offside. This frustrating aspect of play can easily be corrected. When passing and receiving become integral parts of a team's advancing strategy, the potential for blown opportunities diminishes. The Wheel in any of its forms forces players to pass the puck before any offside can occur at the point of attack.

• *After passing a puck, move into open ice.* A common mistake even the best professional players make is to "pass and glide," meaning that once the pass is made the skates stop moving. Don't stop and admire the pass; it can be very unwise if an opponent is lining up for a big hit. Pass and immediately move into an open area to become an outlet target once more. The basic give and go is still one of the best plays in hockey when executed properly.

With advanced players, the Wheel can produce fast-paced, up-tempo practices that players enjoy while refining their skills. In addition, coaches are rewarded for using this drill pattern because less time is lost to setup and transition from drill to drill. Once the basic idea is understood, build on it progressively. This natural sequencing and progression will develop skills and confidence among the players as they move toward mastery of the pattern.

21 Single Wheel

Purpose

- Practice passing and receiving skills using an entry-level wheel format

Equipment   None

Time   Two to three minutes

Procedure

1. Two equal groups of players stand on diagonally opposite sides of the rink.
2. The first player from one group initiates the drill by skating without a puck around the center face-off circle.
3. The first player from the opposite group passes a puck to the skater who then loops back to the same end from which he or she started and finishes with a shot on goal.
4. The passer then skates without a puck toward the other group, receives a pass to make a shot, and so on. Remember to have players switch sides and skate in both directions.

Key Points

- The receiver should keep the stick blade on the ice for easier reception.
- The receiver should call for the puck.
- Passers should never pass behind the intended receiver.

Drill Progressions

- Attempt to have both lines begin at the same time.
- Have players start by skating backward and pivot to forward skating to refine turns and pivots.

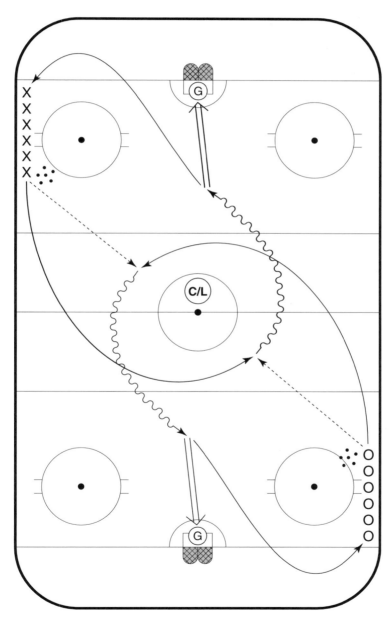

22 2-on-0 Wheel

Purpose

- Reinforce timing and passing skills through the wheel

Equipment   None

Time   Two to three minutes

Procedure

1. Players are in the same starting positions as described in the Single Wheel drill.
2. Two players from the same line skate around the wheel. One player controls the puck while the other skates beside him or her.
3. As both players round the center circle, the player with the puck passes to one of the players in the opposite line who returns the pass.
4. The skaters return to their end with a 2-on-0 scoring situation. Players in the other line initiate their sequence once the pass has been made, and so on, until all players have made a shot on goal.

Key Points

- Provide a target for the return pass.
- Don't cut up ice too quickly! The receiver should skate roughly parallel to the blue line (straight-line skate) when receiving the pass so the passer has a clean target.

Drill Progressions

- Have both groups go at the same time (four players are in motion simultaneously).
- Turn this into a defensive 1-on-1 drill, where the player without the puck attempts to defend against the other skater.

2-on-0 Wheel

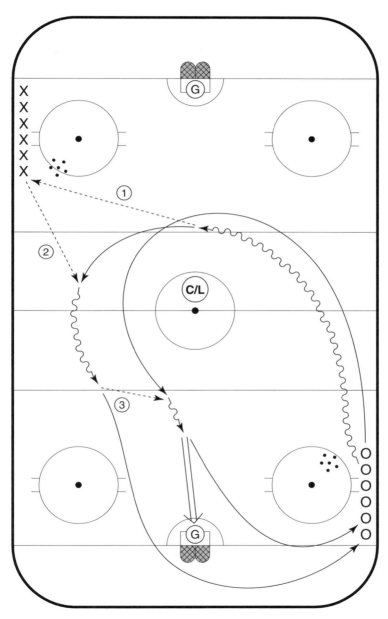

23 Situation Wheel

Purpose

- Practice defending against different offensive situations at the defensive blue line

Equipment   None

Time   Two to three minutes

Procedure

1. Players assume the same group setup as seen in the previous wheel drills.
2. Four players start from one end, with one player acting as the designated defenseman.
3. The defenseman cuts along the center red line and pivots backward to defend a three-player attack.
4. One of the attackers receives the puck from the opposite line, continues toward the opposite goal, and attempts a shot on goal. Once the play is completed, all four players return to their line, rotating the designated defenseman for the next rush.

Key Points

- The defenseman must attempt to create an effective "gap" between him- or herself and the offensive players. The space between the attackers and the defender should be narrow.
- Offensive players can work on setting offensive plays as the puck moves into the zone beyond the blue line.

Drill Progressions

- Change to create a 2-on-2 situation with two defensemen cutting across the red line instead of only one.
- Add an additional offensive player and make it a 3 on 2 out of the wheel.

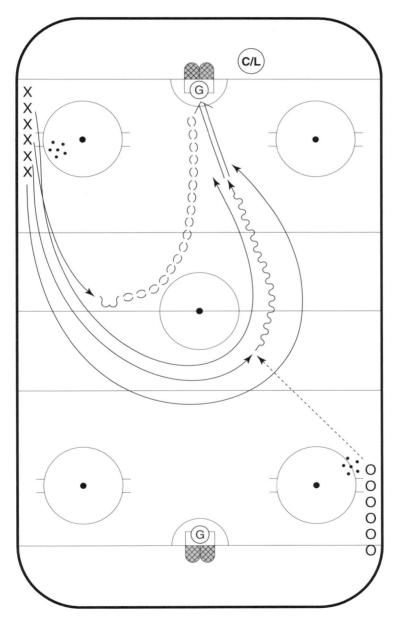

24 Delayed Wheel

Purpose

- Develop passing and receiving skills in conjunction with timing as attackers enter the offensive zone

Equipment Four pylons

Time Two to three minutes

Procedure

1. Players assume basic wheel groups and locations to begin the drill. The four pylons are placed evenly around the center face-off circle.
2. Three players leave one group and prepare to turn back up the ice in a 3-on-0 situation.
3. The first player turns around the closest pylon, the second player cuts through the middle of the pylons, and the third player turns around the furthest pylon.
4. The first player in the second group passes a puck to one of the skaters.
5. Players practice offensive situations based upon different entry times into the offensive zone by the three players.

Key Points

- This drill causes two players to turn roughly at the same time while the player rounding the furthest pylon is delayed. As a result, various offensive opportunities may be attempted.
- Offsides are not allowed, as any player is eligible to receive the pass from the opposite group.

Drill Progressions

- Spread the pylons further apart to create different delays.
- Add a backchecker from the opposite group to add pressure.

Delayed Wheel

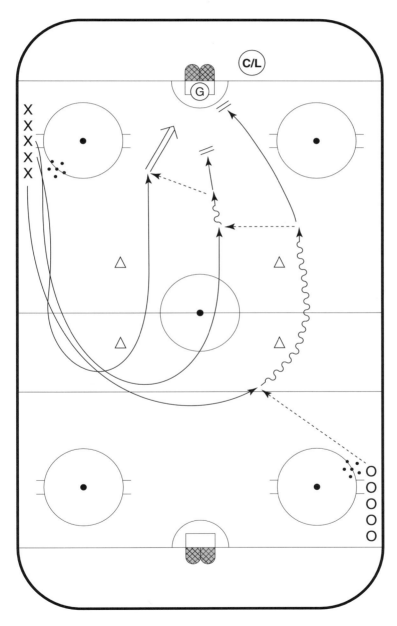

25 Six-Pass Wheel

Purpose

- Refine passing and receiving skills at a high tempo

Equipment   None

Time   Two minutes

Procedure

1. Players are divided equally into four groups and placed in the four corners of the rink.
2. One player begins the drill by skating toward the opposite end of the rink and passing to the first player in the opposite line.
3. The pass is returned to the skater who continues around the center circle as diagrammed, passing to the other groups. The skater finishes by taking a shot on goal.
4. Each group sends a player to do the circuit in succession.

Key Points

- Players skating the circuit must be ready to pass and receive quickly and with accuracy.
- Players must keep their stick blades close to the ice while calling for the puck.

Drill Progressions

- Have players from all groups begin at the same time (four players running the drill simultaneously).
- Add a backward pivot to the drill each time a player passes the center red line with the puck.

Six-Pass Wheel

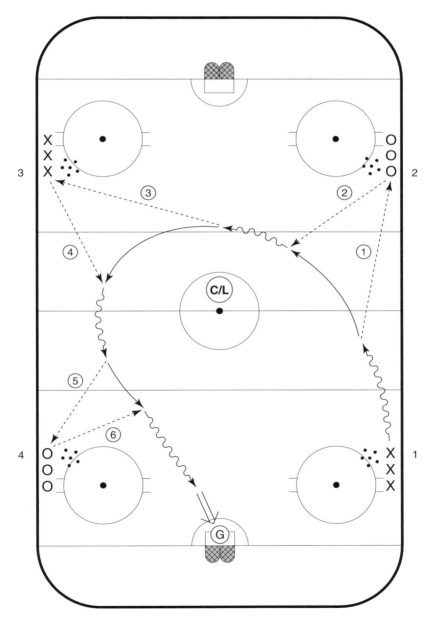

26 Reverse Six-Pass Wheel

Purpose

- Practice and reinforce passing and receiving skills at a high tempo

Equipment   None

Time   Two minutes

Procedure

1. Players are in the same setup as in the Six-Pass Wheel drill.
2. This time, the player beginning the circuit skates in the opposite direction from drill #25, skating toward the opposite diagonal end of the rink instead of directly across. This directional change forces players to use a different pass, either backhand or forehand depending on how they hold their sticks.
3. Complete the circuit the same as in the previous drill with six passes and a shot on goal.

Key Points

- Don't cheat by making the easiest pass, normally the forehand. If the direction the skater is travelling requires backhand passing, even long passes should be completed using a backhand method.

Drill Progressions

- Add a chaser from one of the other groups to simulate gamelike pressure from behind.
- After the shooter has made a shot, have the shooter stay in the goal crease to act as a deflector or screener for the next shot.

Reverse Six-Pass Wheel

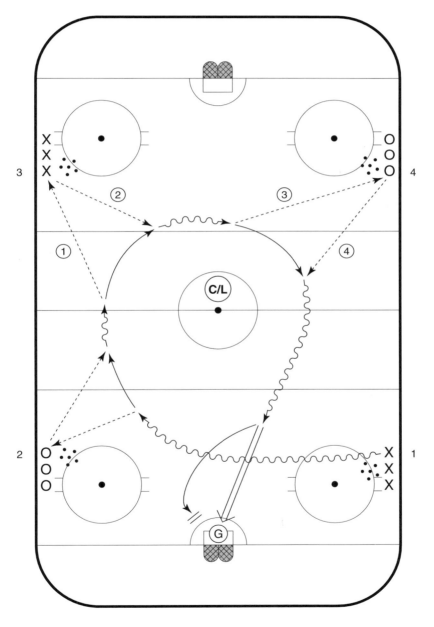

27 Four-Corner Wheel

Purpose

- Simulate a three-player attack up the ice with no pressure

Equipment None

Time Two minutes

Procedure

1. Players are in the same setup as in the previous drill.
2. A player with a puck skates toward the opposite end, passing and receiving with other groups as the player skates around the wheel.
3. After returning the pass to the skater, the other players immediately jump into the play. All three players move toward the opposite end of the rink.
4. Timing becomes an important part of this drill as it is completed with a shot on goal.

Key Points

- Decide when all four groups will take their turn skating with the puck. All players must be ready to join in the attack when needed.
- Players must attempt to complete this drill with their skates in motion the entire time; no gliding is allowed.

Drill Progressions

- Have players from all four groups move simultaneously with one designated as a defenseman or backchecker.
- Add a second puck for the last player in the zone, turning it into a two-shot drill.

Four-Corner Wheel

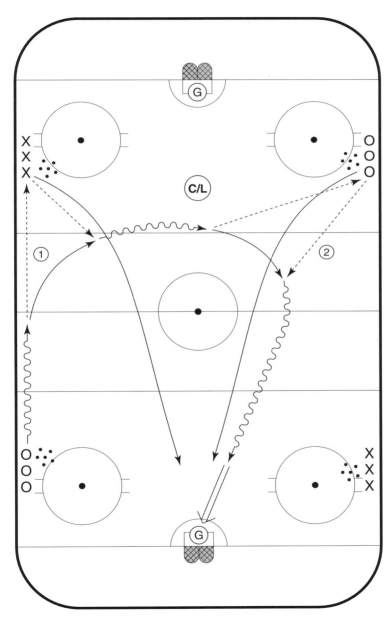

28 Two-Puck Exchange

Purpose

- Practice passing and timing in an overload environment

Equipment None

Time Four to five minutes

Procedure

1. With players located in all four corners, diagonally opposite groups begin at the same time with one player from each group skating forward with a puck.
2. After skating to the near blue line, skaters pass to each other through the neutral zone.
3. After completing these passes, the skaters continue in the wheel loop and pass to the first player in the opposite line. After receiving return passes, skaters finish by taking shots on goal.
4. The other two groups begin the sequence in the other direction.

Key Points

- Skaters must pass ahead of their partners. Any pass behind will affect the flow of the drill.
- This drill requires a little extra time to perfect because passing and receiving under a time constraint is difficult at first.

Drill Progressions

- Once the drill is mastered, players who have exchanged pucks should stop and go in the other direction.
- Add different pivots and turns depending on the ice markings (e.g., pivot at the neutral zone face-off dots).

Two-Puck Exchange

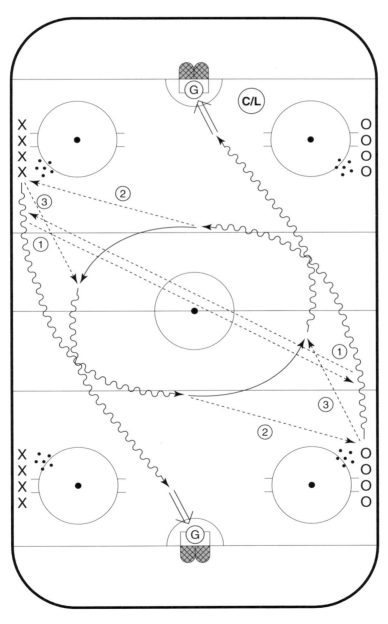

29 Continuous One-Puck Wheel

Purpose

• Develop passing and receiving skills in conjunction with timing

Equipment None

Time One to two minutes

Procedure

1. Players are divided into two groups at diagonally opposite corners of the rink. Each group is split into forwards and defensemen.
2. A forward starts the drill by carrying a puck into the neutral zone and passing it to a defenseman who has skated from the opposite end of the ice.
3. The forward continues around the wheel and receives a return pass from the defenseman. The forward passes to another defenseman who has jumped into the play from the other end of the rink.
4. The one puck is continuously in motion through the neutral zone following the same pattern as the drill continues.
5. A coach passes a second puck to the forward, who takes a shot on goal to finish.

Key Points

• Timing is essential to the success of this drill. Defensemen should not enter the neutral zone until the appropriate moment.

Drill Progressions

• Have a second defenseman turn this into a 1-on-1 drill as the forward attempts the shot.
• Try the drill in both directions.

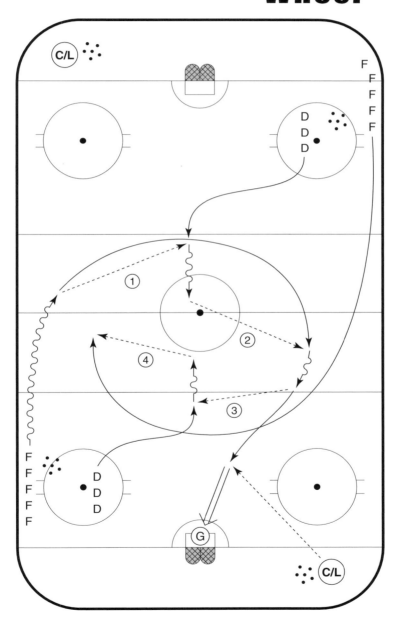

③⓪ Russian Wheel Half-Ice

Purpose

- Use the wheel in a half-ice format

Equipment None

Time Five minutes

Procedure

1. Players are positioned in the same format as the four-wheel activities previously described, only in a smaller space (half-ice).
2. Skating with a puck, a player from the first group passes to the group catty-corner and receives the return pass.
3. The skater goes around the wheel and passes to the second player in his or her original line. The receiver returns the pass to the skater.
4. The skater goes in on goal and finishes with a shot.

Key Points

- Players are in a restricted space and must keep their feet in motion and stick blades on the ice ready for return passes.
- After taking the shot, the skater rotates to another group to work on backhand passing.

Drill Progressions

- Have players pass to all four groups before taking a shot (see diagram).
- Have two players move through the drill at the same time.

Russian Wheel Half-Ice

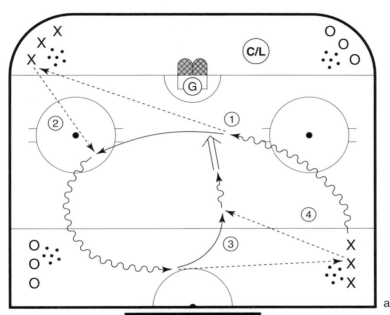

a

Drill Progression

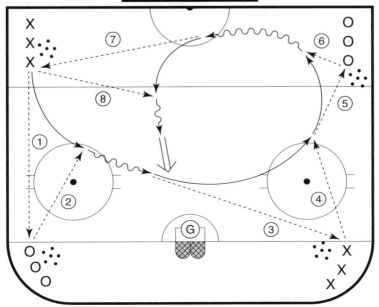

b

Four-Blues Passing and Receiving

The previous chapter demonstrated how a single drill pattern such as the Wheel might be used in a variety of ways. Whether the focus of a given practice is passing and receiving, one-on-one play, or transitions, the Wheel is a valuable tool to include in any practice plan. Similarly, this chapter provides players and coaches with a set of activities that originate in the neutral zone with four groups of players situated in specific locations at both blue lines. These related drills can be sequenced easily to suit a team's unique situation and needs.

Often, coaches and players find that certain practices have no flow to them because of the down time taken up in changing from one drill to the next. New drills require new explanations, which takes time. Four-blues drills do not require extended explanations because one activity flows naturally into the next. This progressive teaching style is a lockstep approach to practice planning and is useful in saving time during practice. In addition, players working on the four-blues drill sequence have greater opportunity to successfully complete these tasks because they understand the basis for the drill to come. The power of feeling successful and fulfilled after attempting a drill should not be underestimated. Players will be hungry for more if they know the drills are do-able!

Cut Pass

While improving passing and receiving skills through the four-blues sequence, players might try to master a difficult passing skill known as the *cut pass*, also commonly referred to as a *saucer pass*. The passer using a cut pass raises a puck over a defenseman's outstretched stick in situations where a pass along the ice will be intercepted or deflected. The trick to executing the cut pass is to begin with the puck at the back of the stick blade toward the heel (figure 5.1). As the pass begins, the puck slides along the stick blade and spins as it gains momentum. A snap of the wrist as the puck exits the blade near the toe lifts the puck slightly off the ice while maintaining a constant saucer shape and position (figure 5.2a). If the cut pass is done properly, the puck will rest flat on the ice with no bouncing (figure 5.2b). Developing this pass takes skill, wrist strength, and a good feel for the stick and puck.

Figure 5.1   Position of the puck on the stick blade before executing a cut pass

Figure 5.2a   Passing and receiving a cut pass. The passer (at far right) is in the process of sending the cut pass

Figure 5.2b Passer and receiver after the cut pass

The following drills represent a variety of passing and receiving objectives. Use the drills to complement conditioning training. Or use these lead-up activities to incorporate transition play as a function of passing and receiving. Whatever the focus, these drills are popular with players of all ages and levels. Be creative while trying these different drills so that you can adapt the drills for a particular group of players.

31 Double Blues

Purpose

- Practice passing and receiving using a standard drill protocol

Equipment   None

Time   Two to three minutes

Procedure

1. Players are in four equal groups situated on the blue lines close to the sideboards on opposite ends of the rink as shown. This standard formation is used throughout the rest of this chapter.
2. One player begins by skating with a puck and passing to the first player in the opposite group on the same side of the ice.
3. The receiver passes to the first player in the group immediately across the rink while the skater continues in a looping pattern as shown in the diagram.
4. The puck is returned to the skater, who completes the drill with a shot on goal. The passer, from the group diagonally across the rink, then begins the sequence again. The other two groups take their turns in succession.

Key Points

- Players must make crisp, accurate passes and call for the puck.
- The skater must attempt to keep his or her skates in motion throughout the drill.

Drill Progressions

- Have opposite lines start at the same time, meaning that two players go at once.
- Have the coach pass a second puck from the corner for a second shot opportunity.
- Add a backchecker from one of the lines to create a pressure drill.

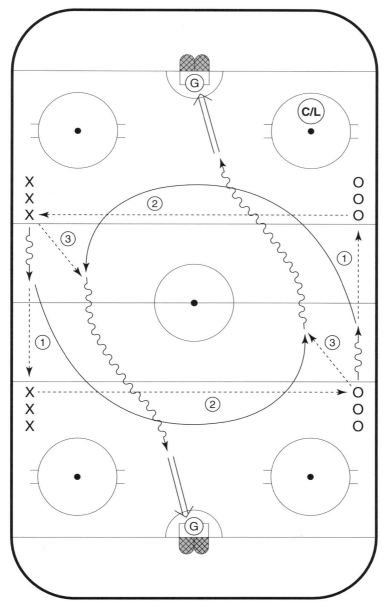

32 Back It Up

Purpose

- Practice passing and receiving in conjunction with stopping, pivoting, and other skating skills

Equipment   None

Time   Two to three minutes

Procedure

1. Players are in the standard four-blues formation.
2. At the whistle, players from diagonally opposite lines skate toward the far side of the center face-off circle at the red line and stop.
3. The players skate backward around the circle, moving toward their original groups.
4. The skaters pivot to skate forward, head up the ice, and receive a pass from the first player in the group across the rink, finishing with a shot on goal. Players from the other two groups begin on the next whistle.

Key Points

- Players must wait for the coach's whistle to make sure that each pair has open ice in which to work, avoiding confusion and possible injury.
- The Back It Up drill is a thinking drill as well, forcing players to look for their routes and listen to their passing or receiving assignments.

Drill Progressions

- Change where the players must stop and move in different directions.
- Modify to include two players coming at once from the same group with different assignments.

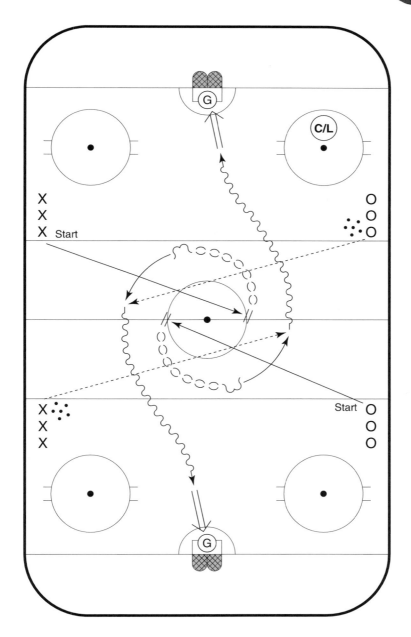

33 Cross-Ice Leads

Purpose

- Practice puck control, passing, and receiving at breakaway speeds
- Reinforce proper timing for long passes

Equipment   None

Time   Two to three minutes

Procedure

1. Players are in the standard four-blues formation.
2. One player from the first two catty-corner groups breaks through the neutral zone toward the far blue line.
3. As the skaters approach their respective blue lines, players from opposite lines feed long passes to the skaters.
4. The skaters go in for a shot, and the passers become the next set of skaters.

Key Points

- Passers must be onside with the stick blade and puck within the neutral zone.
- Receivers should stay onside at the far blue line, delaying if necessary to receive the pass rather than going offside.

Drill Progressions

- Turn the passer from each line into a backchecker for the closest puck carrier, creating a pressure situation. The checker would continue the drill as the next skater.

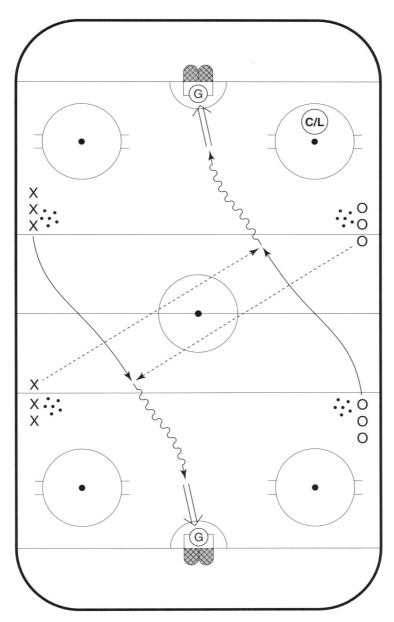

34 Four-Blues Drop

Purpose

- Refine the skill of dropping a pass behind to a trailing teammate

Equipment   None

Time   Four to five minutes per set

Procedure

1. Players are in the standard four-blues formation.
2. One player from a group passes to the first player in the group diagonally opposite on the other side of the rink.
3. The receiver skates a slight loop toward mid-ice along the blue line when receiving the pass, then turns toward the net.
4. The passer follows to receive a drop pass inside the offensive blue line and shoots to complete the drill.
5. Players from the remaining two lines start the sequence again moving toward the other end of the rink.

Key Points

- Receivers should "belly" skate (skate in a relatively tight semi-circle) as diagrammed to make the initial reception easier.
- Passers should avoid putting a "tail" on the drop pass. Passers should not just leave the puck for the receiver; they must make a hard pass.

Drill Progressions

- Create a 2-on-2 situation by adding a backchecker from each group that is not yet involved. One checker will attempt to contain the passer, while the other checker trails the late player.

Four-Blues Drop

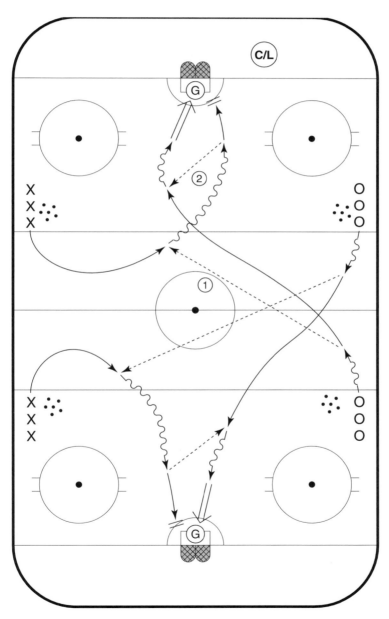

35 Maine 2 on 0

Purpose

- Develop timing and breakaway speed through the neutral zone

Equipment   None

Time   Three to four minutes

Procedure

1. Players are in the standard four-blues formation. Groups on the same sideboards will work together and always skate toward the same end.
2. One player skates through the neutral zone, roughly along the blue line as shown, and accepts a pass from the first player in the group catty-corner to the skater's original group.
3. As the skater loops to receive the pass, a player from the other group on the same sideboard as the skater's group skates aggressively toward the far blue line.
4. The puck carrier passes to the breaking player, making sure not to go offside. The pass must be timed so that the receiver accepts the puck just before entering the attack zone.
5. The players complete a 2 on 0, then switch to opposite lines at their end of the rink.

Key Points

- This drill is all about timing and speed. All players must learn to think while skating 100 percent!
- Players must make passes quickly. They should avoid holding onto the puck, as this defeats the purpose of transition through the speed of attack.

Progressive Drills

- Add a defenseman from one of the other lines to make it a 2 on 1.
- Start the activity with backward skating or mandatory pivots.
- Have one of the two attacking players become a backchecker for the next play.

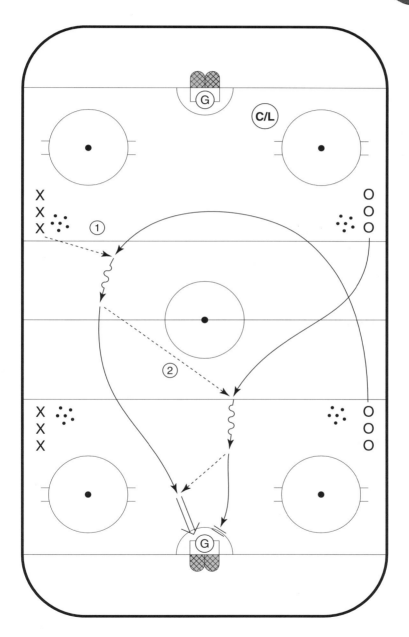

36 Give and Go

Purpose

- Improve foot and hand speed and coordination through a high-tempo passing and receiving activity

Equipment   None

Time   Two to three minutes

Procedure

1. Players are in the standard four-blues formation.
2. At the coach's whistle, two players, each from diagonally opposite groups, pass to the group directly across the ice.
3. After the the first player in the receiving group returns the puck, the skater turns toward the opposite end of the ice, sending another pass to the closest group.
4. After receiving another return pass, the skater goes in for a shot on goal.

Key Points

- Players must wait for the coach's whistle to begin so as to avoid confusion or injury.
- Passes should be executed as fast as possible, with one-time passing and receiving being the preferred method (see chapter 7).

Drill Progressions

- Have the skater pivot or turn to skate backward once, then twice during the sequence.
- Turn this into a deke drill where all "shots" are dekes only, working on that great move in tight on the goalie.

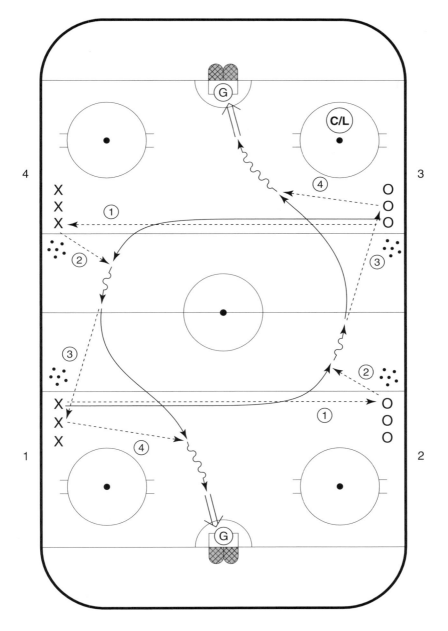

⚡37 Blues Bombs

Purpose

- Practice timing patterns in relation to passing through the neutral zone

Equipment   None

Time   Two to three minutes

Procedure

1. Players are in the standard four-blues formation.
2. One player begins the sequence by passing a puck to the first player in the group opposite along the same sideboards. The passer skates a loop around the middle face-off circle and heads back.
3. The receiver passes to the first player in the group directly across the ice and accepts the return pass.
4. Last, the puck is passed back to the skater, who receives the puck before entering the offensive zone to make a shot on goal.

Key Points

- Timing is key. The skater must "throttle down" if an errant pass is made, remembering to stay onside until the completion of the drill.
- Passes should be hard and accurate so that the skater is not forced to slow the pace of the drill. This is a high-tempo activity!

Drill Progressions

- Provide a second-shot opportunity. Have a coach located in either end pass a second puck.
- Send two players at once, one as a defenseman, making it a high-speed chase to the net.

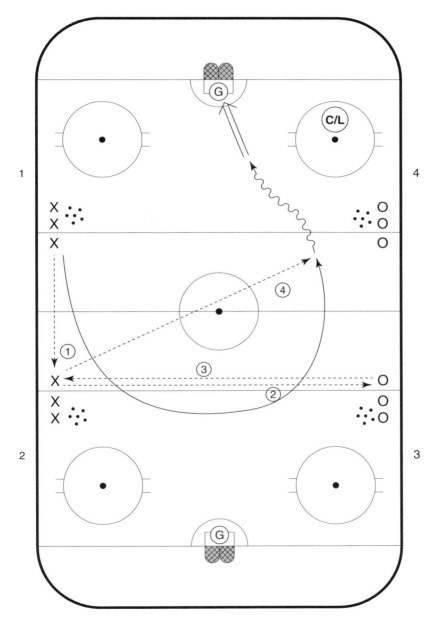

38 Pivot Heaven

Purpose

- Practice passing and receiving while attempting to pivot both forward and backward

Equipment None

Time Two to three minutes

Procedure

1. Players are in the standard four-blues formation.
2. Two players from diagonally opposite lines begin the sequence by passing across the ice to an opposite group member.
3. After receiving the return pass, the player pivots to backward skating and passes once again to the same player.
4. After receiving the second return pass, the player pivots forward and goes in for a shot on goal. The passer then begins the sequence again, and the opposite two groups follow the rotation.

Key Points

- This activity takes practice. The accuracy of all passes is essential so that the flow of the drill isn't slowed or broken.
- Players should remember to keep the stick blade close to the ice to avoid missing return passes.

Drill Progressions

- Add another pass to the adjacent line as the skater enters the offensive zone.
- Have the skater skate deep into the corner and cut back along the goal line to the front of the net, making this a drill where goalies must defend an attack out of the corner.

Pivot Heaven

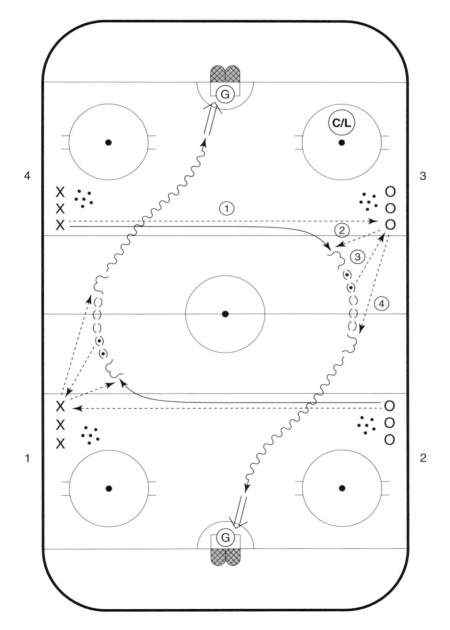

39 2-on-0 Delay

Purpose

- Develop proper timing and improve passing and receiving skills through the neutral zone

Equipment   None

Time   Two to three minutes

Procedure

1. Players are in the standard four-blues formation.
2. One player passes to a player in the group opposite along the same sideboards, then skates the route as shown.
3. The puck is passed once across the ice between the nonskating groups before being returned to the skater.
4. At the same time, a player from the group directly across the ice from the skater's group begins to skate slowly up the ice, then pivots and heads in the same direction as the oncoming skater.
5. The two skaters move in on a 2 on 0 and complete the drill with a shot.

Key Points

- Timing is again critical in this drill, with the second skater delaying his or her start until the appropriate moment.
- Remember, skaters should always pivot toward the play. They should not turn away from the puck carrier.

Drill Progressions

- Send two players from the first line and make the drill a 3 on 0, or a 2 on 1.
- Keep the two skaters in front of the goalie to set up a screen or deflection for the next attack.

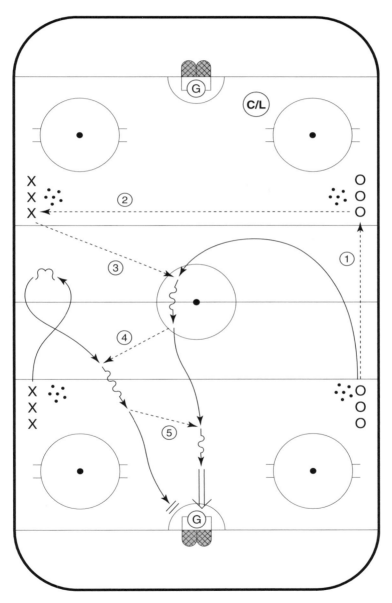

40 Double Escape

Purpose

- Work on pivoting, turning, and breakaway speed within a passing and receiving drill

Equipment Four pylons

Time Two to three minutes

Procedure

1. Players are in the standard four-blues formation. Pylons are placed near the top of each face-off circle in both ends (four pylons total).
2. On the coach's whistle, two players from groups directly across the ice from each other, one with a puck, the other without, begin skating backward around the pylons.
3. As the players pivot forward to skate up the ice, the puck carrier passes to the other skater.
4. A second pass comes from another group member to the player who made the first pass to his or her teammate.
5. Both skaters now have a puck and complete the drill by shooting, one after the other.

Key Points

- Remember, never shoot two pucks at the goalie at the same time. Make sure some separation exists between the shooters so the goalie can effectively play them both.
- Rotate so everyone has a chance to backward skate and pivot with a puck.

Drill Progressions

- Add another pass from a coach in the corner, creating a three-shot drill where goalies must quickly change angles.

Double Escape

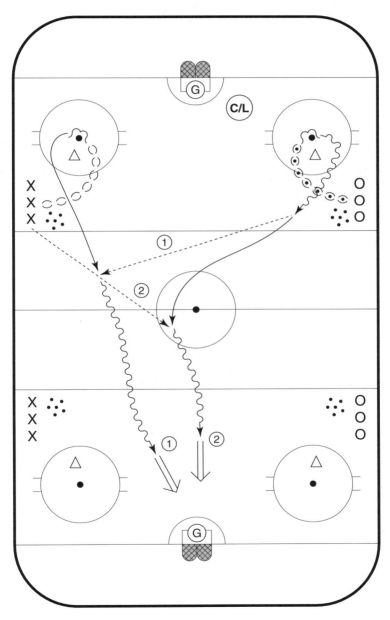

6 High-Speed Puck Movement

"You can't get there as fast as the puck can!" How often have you heard this classic coaches' refrain? This statement is normally reserved for a player who decides to attempt the end-to-end rush while teammates stand by idly and watch. Often, those teammates are open and in position to advance the puck if a pass should come their way. Speed has become an important component of the modern game—speed in skating and in passing and receiving. By increasing the speed of passes and receptions, players also improve their overall game. The notion that "speed kills" is germane to virtually any sport, none more so than hockey.

Nothing is more discouraging for an opponent than to face a team that is skilled in moving the puck quickly while attacking at high speed. The opponent thinks he or she has eliminated all options by closing off the attack lane when suddenly someone feathers a beautifully placed pass onto the stick of a teammate who goes in for a grade-A scoring opportunity. Speed, in virtually all sports and at all positions, can be the difference between success and failure. Reinforce the development of speed through up-tempo practice in passing and receiving drills, as players' skills warrant.

Many coaches and players visualize passing and receiving as a fairly standard, concrete skill set. A skilled player, however, can use increased passing and receiving speed in a variety of ways, some of which are listed next:

• *Use an indirect method of passing, either off the sideboards or through wide rim plays in either the offensive or defensive zones.* Not all passes need go tape to tape as previously described. Often the tempo of play can be increased by passing into a zone where a teammate can retrieve the puck while attacking at full speed instead of having to slow down to receive and carry the puck. Indirect passing can be accomplished by passing behind a teammate on an angle off the sideboards. The receiver then skates hard to retrieve the puck. *Wide rim* refers to a pass shot around the corners in either the defensive or offensive zone. Many coaches refer to a *soft wide rim*, which means that a passer will take a little speed off a wide rim pass to give a teammate time to skate to the boards and set up to receive the puck. In both instances, passes are directed to zones or areas, not the blade of a teammate's stick. Indirect passes can provide immediate, effective outlet options when an opponent is applying pressure.

• *Differentiate between reading control versus reading pressure (time and space, respectively, as they relate to passing).* We have emphasized the importance of players who are away from the puck moving into open ice to become outlet options. Likewise, a player with the puck must also make situational judgments related to passing and receiving. *Reading control* means that a player has time to set up, control the puck, and pass on his or her own time. A good example of reading control occurs during a power play. Possession is key and controlled passes are made only when they favor the team making the power play. Players work hard to get the puck, so they should not be anxious to get rid of it if they don't have to! *Reading pressure* refers to a player's ability to make a safe outlet pass under pressure. This ability ties in nicely with the wide rim concept. A player who can anticipate pressure will have time to plan an escape. Reading control and pressure represents a mental approach to passing and receiving, with preparation and "ice vision" as prerequisites to success.

• *Improve transition skills.* One of the easiest ways to increase the speed of a hockey game is to improve the execution of transitions. For our purposes, *transition* refers to the transfer of puck possession in or near the neutral zone (between the two blue lines) from a defensive to an offensive or attack position. Quick, accurate passes after a turnover create opportunities for entering the attack area. Remember that the puck can get to a target a lot faster than can the passer! Transition is a great application of this concept. A player who holds onto the puck in transitional situations slows down the pace. Holding onto the puck gives opponents time to get into defensive positions and thwart any offensive chances. Passing and receiving the puck quickly and accurately in transitional situations increase speed and scoring chances.

• *Pass with some oomph!* The greatest difference between players in the National Hockey League (NHL) and players at lower levels is the greater speed in the NHL, especially in passing. Most NHL players pass the puck crisply and with authority. All players should attempt hard passes as early as possible because soft passes with no oomph are more likely to be intercepted or miss the target. Sometimes a soft, feathery pass is required for a specific game situation, but the majority of passes should be firm and on target as quickly as possible. Practice to make hard passes automatic.

The following drills force players to pass and receive at high speed. Included are several drills designed for offensive zone play where speed is essential in getting to open areas for timely scoring opportunities. Remember that speed must also be generated when there isn't a lot of room. Some of the drills force players to work on quickness as a function of overall speed. Challenging players to go "flat out" in drills pushes their limits and increases their abilities to exploit an opponent's weaknesses. Although these drills can be adapted for almost all levels, players should first possess basic passing and receiving skills. The sooner players combine passing and receiving with speed, however, the sooner they can dominate and more fully enjoy this exciting aspect of the game.

41 Dartmouth Drill

Purpose

- Practice passing, receiving, and shooting with space and time restrictions

Equipment None

Time Four to five minutes total

Procedure

1. Players are divided into two equal groups located along either sideboard near the hash marks. One player from each group is positioned along the goal line as a give-and-go passer.
2. The first player in one group passes to the player along the goal line and skates quickly toward the net; he or she then receives a return pass and takes a shot. The player then skates to the back of the opposite group.
3. Once the first shot has been taken, a player from the other group repeats the procedure in the opposite direction.

Key Points

- Players must wait until the shooter from the opposite group has cleared the front of the net before beginning their sequence.
- The key is to develop quick feet and hands for scoring chances in tight to the goal.

Drill Progressions

- Attempt to make this a one-time passing situation.
- Have players from both groups moving at once, where the player without the puck looks for a quick cross-ice pass or rebound off the shot (see diagram).

Dartmouth Drill 41

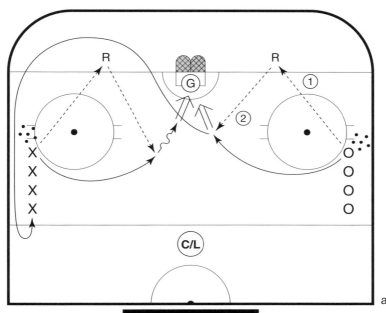

a

Drill Progression

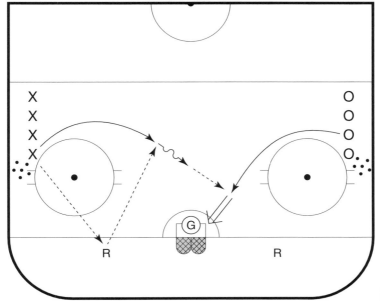

b

111

42 St. John Pass and Shot

Purpose

- Practice passing and receiving at a high tempo while changing direction

Equipment   None

Time   Two to three minutes

Procedure

1. Players are in one of four groups located at either blue line near the face-off dots or along the goal line as shown in the diagram.
2. The drill is done in an alternating fashion, one side after the other.
3. A player at the blue line makes a pass to his or her partner located at the goal line; the player skates, pivots, and receives a return pass.
4. The player then skates a loop around the blue line group and goes in for a shot on goal. Once finished, the two players switch lines as the other groups begin the drill again from the other side of the ice.

Key Points

- Do not turn away as the puck is passed. Always pivot to face the puck.
- Attempt to make crisp, tape-to-tape passes. Thereafter, skate to the net as quickly as possible to finish the drill.

Drill Progressions

- Skate a wider route (see diagram), or add a second passer from the other groups.

St. John Pass and Shot

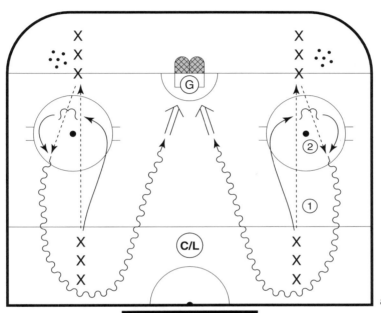

a

Drill Progression

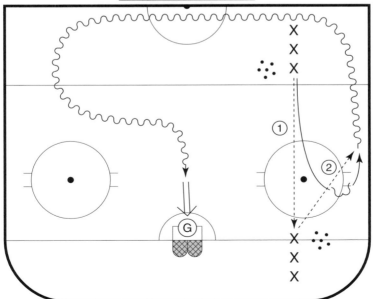

b

43 Double Give and Go

Purpose

- Practice short, accurate passing and receiving at a high tempo

Equipment None

Time Three to four minutes

Procedure

1. This drill begins in a setup that is similar to the previous setup in drill #42. Only one player, however, is positioned near the blue line to act as an outlet passer.
2. A player begins by passing to the outlet passer, then skates quickly around that player while preparing for a return pass.
3. Once the puck is returned, the player makes a second pass to the last player in line in the original group of players in the corner and that player makes a second return pass.
4. After completing the drill with a shot the player proceeds to the back of the line in the opposite group.

Key Points

- Rotating the outlet passer every five passes will keep everyone active and alert, ready to assume that position when called to do so.
- Remember that this drill should develop quick, accurate passes at high speeds where possible. Keep the tempo from slowing down by urging players to pass and receive quickly.

Drill Progressions

- Have the initial player pass through both groups of players in either corner, resulting in up to eight short passes (see diagram). Add a player who will "chase," giving pressure from behind.

Double Give and Go

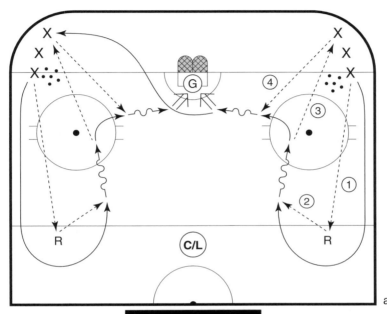

a

Drill Progression

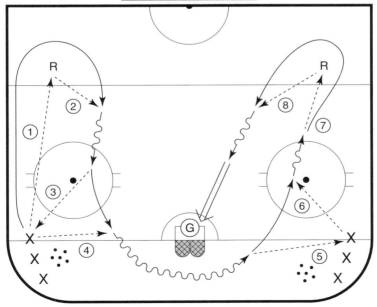

b

44 Quarterback

Purpose

- Practice passing and receiving, direct and indirect, originating behind the offensive goal

Equipment   None

Time   Three to four minutes

Procedure

1. Forwards are in two equal groups in either corner of one end of the ice. Defensemen are along the blue line, two per drill.
2. Forward 1 (F^1) carries the puck behind the net, stops, then passes off the boards to either defenseman. F^1 continues to the front of the net to act as a screen or rebounder. Forward 2 (F^2) loops around a face-off circle and goes to the net for a pass or rebound.
3. A defenseman takes a shot or passes to either forward. One rebound is played, then players return to their respective lines.

Key Points

- F^1 must judge the proper angle for passing off the boards to a defenseman not in position to receive the puck.
- After an initial walk-through at a slow pace, increase the tempo, simulating a game situation.

Drill Progressions

- Use only one defenseman who must be ready to move toward either sideboard quickly to retrieve a pass off the boards (see diagram).
- The passer can elect to pass indirectly or directly to the defenseman from behind the net.

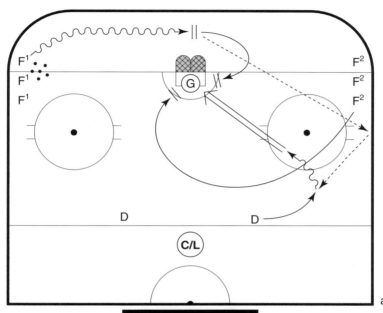

a

Drill Progression

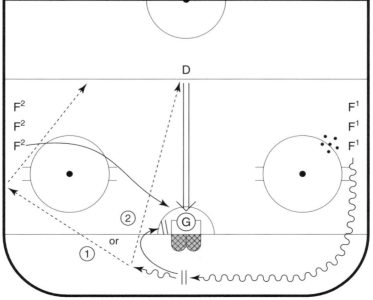

b

45 Dot Sprint

Purpose

- Practice passing and receiving through the neutral zone while straight-line skating

Equipment   None

Time   Three to four minutes

Procedure

1. Players are in one group located along the center red line. If a half-ice format is used, two equal groups use opposite ends.
2. A player leaves one end of the line and performs a tight turn around a neutral zone face-off dot. The next player in line passes a puck as the skater comes out of the turn.
3. The skater returns the puck to the last player in line at the opposite end of the group, receives a return pass, and makes a tight turn around the other face-off dot in the neutral zone.
4. The skater finishes with a shot on goal. The last passer from the end of the line begins the drill from the opposite direction.

Key Points

- The skater should skate in a fairly straight line, staying close to the blue line. This positioning gives the passers a good target.
- As with many of the other drills, high-tempo, successful passes and receptions demonstrate mastery of these skills.

Drill Progressions

- Have the skater turn around the face-off dots in the offensive zone as well, completing the drill at high speed (see diagram).

Dot Sprint 45

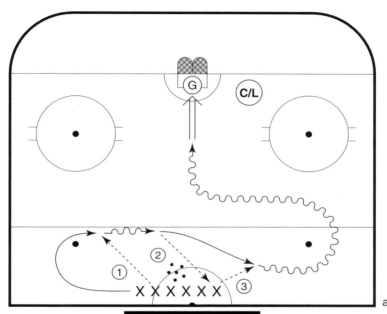

a

Drill Progression

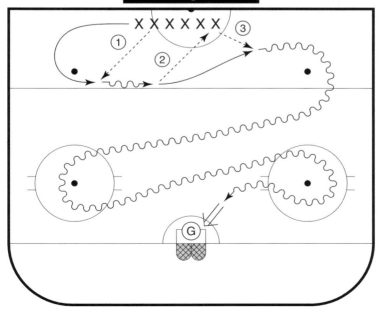

b

119

46 Revolver

Purpose

- Practice passing and receiving using tight turn skating skills at high speed

Equipment   None

Time   Three to four minutes

Procedure

1. Players are divided into two equal groups at either sideboard near the center red line.
2. The first player in line skates with a puck around the center face-off circle at high speed.
3. The skater passes to the first player in the opposite line who immediately returns the pass. The skater passes to the next player in line in the skater's original group. The skater receives the return pass.
4. The skater goes in for a shot on goal to complete the drill.

Key Points

- After returning the pass, the player in the opposite group begins the drill in the opposite direction. The Revolver is a continuous drill.
- The stick blade should never leave the ice during this activity.

Drill Progressions

- Have players pivot while skating around the center face-off circle, moving from forward to backward skating, then forward again.
- Add a coach at either end to provide a second puck for practicing dekes on the goalies.

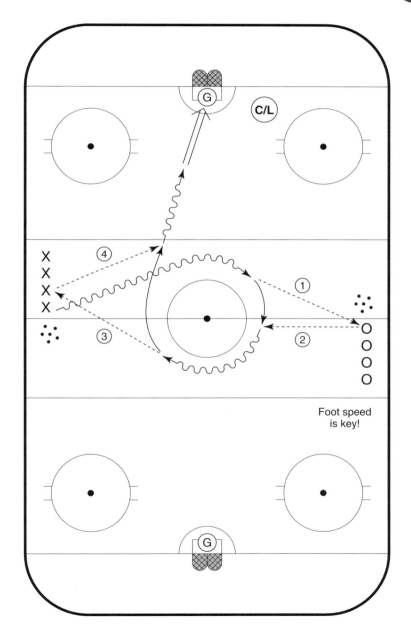

C/L

Foot speed
is key!

47 High Octane

Purpose

- To force players to keep their feet moving while passing and receiving at top speed

Equipment   None

Time   Two to three minutes

Procedure

1. Players are in two groups as seen in the previous drill (#46) along either sideboard. Additional players are situated at each face-off dot in either end zone (four players total).
2. At the whistle, one player from each group leaves, skates around the center circle, and receives a pass from a player in the opposite group.
3. The skater passes to and receives a return pass from the player at the end face-off dot. The skater continues around the net and passes to the player at the next face-off dot, loops around the face-off circle, and comes in for a shot on goal.
4. The next player in either group leaves on the coach's whistle. The four stationary passers are changed every ten whistles.

Key Points

- Players can go only at the whistle to avoid potential mid-ice collisions or injuries.
- Players should keep their feet moving at all times, especially when emerging from behind the net.

Drill Progressions

- After taking a shot, the shooter remains close to the net to act as a screen or tipper for the next shot. Leave up to three players to create a difficult situation for the goalies.
- Try a 2-on-0 situation, in which one player from the opposite line joins the rush late for a second shooting option.

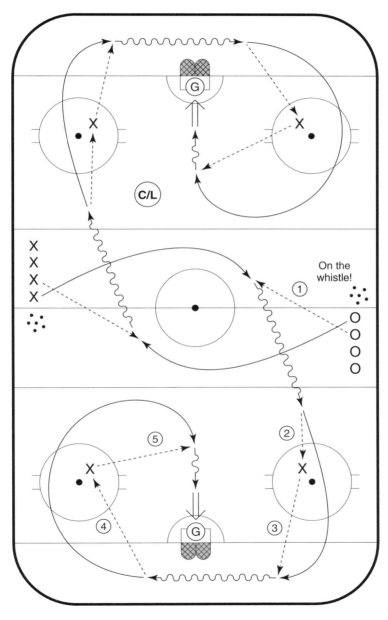

48 Indirect Break

Purpose

- Teach players to use the boards to pass indirectly at high speed

Equipment None

Time Three to four minutes

Procedure

1. Players are in four groups in the four corners of the rink.
2. On the whistle, two players from one end skate forward, one with a puck, one without.
3. The skater with the puck makes a long pass slightly behind his or her partner, who retrieves it off the sideboard. At the same time, the second player in the line where the skater without a puck began makes the same type of long pass across the ice to the skater who made the first pass.
4. Both skaters take shots on goal at the opposite end of the ice. The coach blows the whistle to signal two players from the other end to begin the drill, moving toward the opposite end.

Key Points

- Passers must learn the right angles so that the pass lands on the receiver's stick blade.
- Perform this drill at flat-out speed.

Drill Progressions

- Both skaters begin with pucks and make long sideboard passes at the same time.
- Use defensemen in the neutral zone, and turn this into two separate 1-on-1 plays.

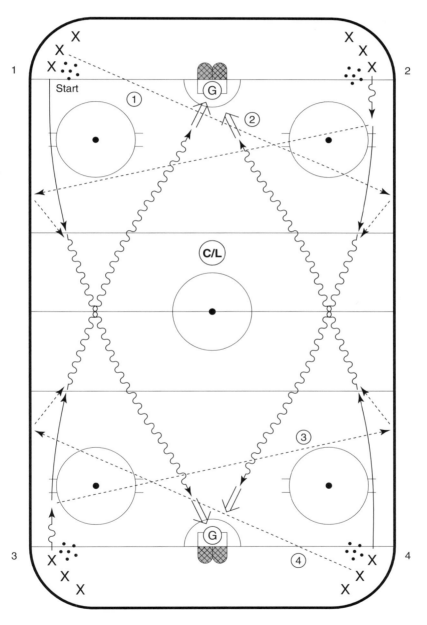

49 Pass to Zones Transition

Purpose

- Reinforce timing and quick passes through the middle of the neutral zone

Equipment   None

Time   Four to five minutes

Procedure

1. Defensemen are in two equal groups along the sideboards near the center red line. Forwards are in two equal groups near the blue line sideboards.
2. A defenseman skates forward into the offensive zone, pivots, and skates backward toward the far boards. As the defenseman nears the red line, he or she pivots to skate forward and receives a pass from a forward in the closest group.
3. A forward from the opposite group times the play so that as the defenseman receives the first pass, the forward moves quickly along the blue line into the attacking zone.
4. The defenseman passes quickly to the forward who goes in for a shot on goal.

Key Points

- Forwards must be patient and not start too soon; they must avoid offside plays.
- After receiving the pass, defensemen must move the puck as quickly as possible to the breaking forward.

Drill Progressions

- Have the defenseman follow up with a second puck for a screen or tip opportunity (see diagram).
- Have the forward who makes the first pass move into the zone for a second-chance shot.

Pass to Zones Transition

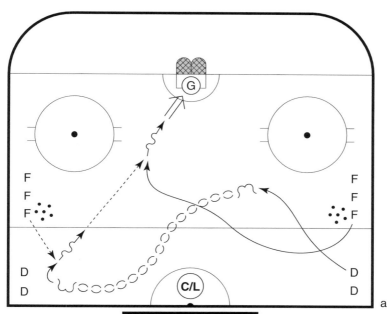

a

Drill Progression

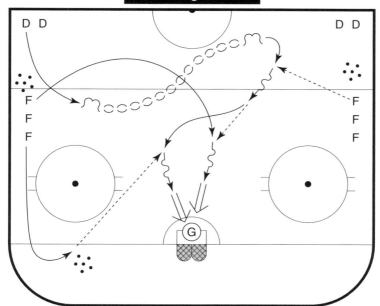

b

⑤⓪ Pass Conditioner

Purpose

- Refine passing and receiving while skating forward or backward at top speed
- Add a conditioning element to practice

Equipment   None

Time   Four to five minutes

Procedure

1. Players are in four groups near the goal line. Each group has four pucks.
2. At the whistle, the first player from each group takes a puck and skates backward toward the near blue line. The skater passes to the next player in line while continuing to skate backward.
3. After receiving a return pass, the skater leaves the puck on the near blue line and races back to his or her group. The skater picks up a second puck and carries it to the near blue line while backward skating.
4. The process continues until all four pucks are on the blue line. The next player in line skates forward to the near blue line to retrieve a puck, passes to the next person in line, and receives a return pass while forward skating. The second skater deposits the puck on the goal line.

Key Points

- Keep the stick blade on the ice. Resist the temptation to raise it, especially as fatigue sets in.
- Go at top speed to deliver all four pucks. Work on pivoting at the same time.

Drill Progressions

- Add a second set where players must skate to the red line. Add a third set where players must go to the far blue line or the opposite goal line.

Pass Conditioner

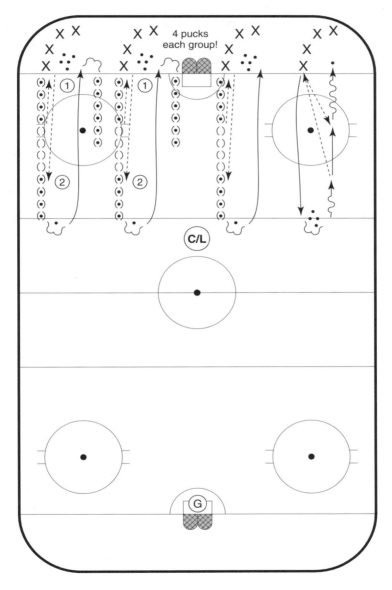

7) One-Time or Touch Passes

So far we have focused on passing and receiving mechanics that players must refine into an automatic skill set. In the last chapter, we added speed, increasing the difficulty of these skills. At this point, players should have the necessary passing and receiving techniques down to a science.

Now, let's take these skills to the next level!

Highly skilled athletes in any sport eventually learn to increase their game speed by increasing the pace at which they execute skills. Think of Barry Sanders, the great football running back, cutting into a hole created by the offensive line, moving through just before the lane collapses. He has learned to read and react quicker than most, producing consistently great runs. Or picture former National Basketball Association star Michael Jordan sliding by a defender off a play designed for the famous Chicago Bulls triangle offense. Even when the defense knew the play was coming, Jordan's ability to beat his defender to a spot allowed him to be successful time after time. Fans watching these players often ask, "How did that happen so fast?" or "Where did that player come from?" Similarly, in hockey the increased attack speed of players like Yzerman, Modano, or Hull often results from increased passing and receiving speed. To move players' skill level up a notch, they must perfect one-time or touch passing.

"Touch passing" and "touch receiving" imply that the player merely touches the puck as it is passed rather than receiving and cradling it. The objective is to redirect the puck to a teammate or area without holding the puck for any length of time. A perfect example of touch or one-time passing is during a breakout. A defenseman passes the puck to a breaking center curling through the middle of the ice preparing to break out of the zone. At that same moment, a rival defenseman elects to "take away ice" and moves forward in an attempt to break up the play. This would be a perfect time for the center to merely touch pass

to a breaking winger before the opponent has time to react, allowing the breakout to continue.

Often a touch pass does not have to be tape to tape. Simply moving the puck into an open area for a teammate to retrieve often gets the job done and provides open ice. The key is quickness, not necessarily accuracy. Of course, in the offensive zone, a one-time shot off of a one-time pass can be a deadly combination. In these instances, more exactness and accuracy is a must and takes years and years to perfect. Players shouldn't get discouraged if their touch passing does not measure up to expectations as soon as they would like.

Let's cover one last technique before moving into the drills. To execute an effective one-time pass, the lower arms, wrists, and fingers must be prepared and slightly more rigid than normal. Players don't want to "give with the puck" when receiving it as they normally would. They should be careful, however, not to squeeze the stick too firmly or they will end up with little directional control as the puck rebounds off the blade. Players should experiment to determine the exact amount of force needed in the arms, hands, and stick shaft.

The following drills incorporate high-tempo passing and receiving skills while reducing the amount of time players actually spend with the puck on their stick blades. Players executing these drills need to make judgments at higher speeds than that to which they might be accustomed, thereby learning to handle the gamelike complications of time pressure. At first, these drills may seem difficult or confusing to younger or less skilled players. Players who are able to complete these drills properly, however, enhance their chances of being successful in games. One-time passing can be a deadly new weapon in the team's offensive arsenal, but be prepared to spend countless hours refining this difficult skill.

51 One-Touch Warm-Up

Purpose

- Introduce one-touch passing

Equipment   None

Time   Two to three minutes

Procedure

1. Players are in three groups on both sides of the rink close to the sideboards as diagrammed, with one group on the near blue line, one group close to the face-off circle hash marks, and one group on the goal line.
2. The first player from the blue line group skates forward with the puck and passes to the first player in line near the hash marks. The receiver uses a one-touch pass to return the puck to the skater. The skater completes a second one-touch pass to the first player in the group along the goal line.
3. The skater finishes by taking a one-time shot on the goalie, then rotates to the goal line group.
4. After the shot, a skater from the opposite side of the rink begins, and the drill continues.

Key Points

- Wait until the shot is taken before initiating the drill from the opposite corner.
- This is a precision drill, not a speed drill. Work on proper technique to ensure effective one-time passes.

Drill Progressions

- Increase the speed or number of passes in this relatively restricted space (see diagram).
- Try using backhand passes and receptions as well.

One-Touch Warm-Up

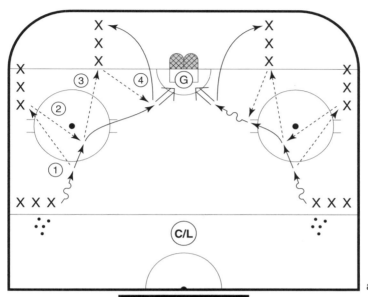

a

Drill Progression

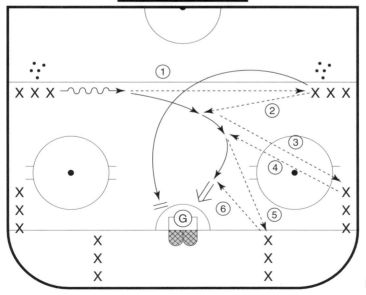

b

52 Tiger Shark

Purpose

- Practice one-touch passing in open-ice situations

Equipment   None

Time   Two to three minutes

Procedure

1. Players are in three groups. Two groups are in the corners of the rink at the same end of the ice; one group is at the center circle.
2. A player from one of the corner groups skates forward with a puck. The skater passes to the first player in the center group who executes a one-time return pass then begins skating around the center circle.
3. The skater takes a shot on goal at the far end of the rink. The skater retrieves the puck from the corner and passes to the player from the center group who has completed skating around the center circle.
4. The puck carrier passes to the second corner group, receives a one-time return pass, and takes a shot on goal.
5. The drill continues, this time from the opposite corner line.

Key Points

- The first shooter rotates to the center group after making his or her outlet pass.
- Timing and accuracy are key to the successful completion of this drill.

Drill Progressions

- Add a chaser at one or two points in the drill, forcing the offensive players to speed up the tempo.

Tiger Shark 52

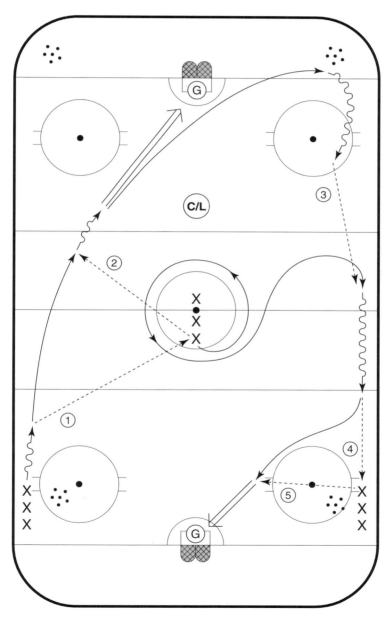

53 Ranger Drill

Purpose

- Attempt difficult long-distance, one-time passes
- Force players to "think the drill"

Equipment   None

Time   Three to four minutes

Procedure

1. Players are in two groups near the face-off circles in diagonally opposite ends of the ice and along the sideboards as diagrammed.
2. At the whistle, the first player from each group skates across the ice and cuts up the ice toward the blue line and the opposite end of the rink as he or she nears the sideboards.
3. The next player in each group passes to the closest skater on the same side of the ice. The pass is one-time returned.
4. The skaters skate back across the ice between the red and blue lines and receive passes from their original groups.
5. Both skaters skate to the opposite end of the rink to complete the drill with a shot on goal.

Key Points

- Ideally, and if the timing works well, the third pass is one-timed as well. Both skaters pass then immediately look to receive.
- This drill reinforces the old coaching axiom, "Don't admire your pass too long!"

Drill Progressions

- Have four groups alternate sides.

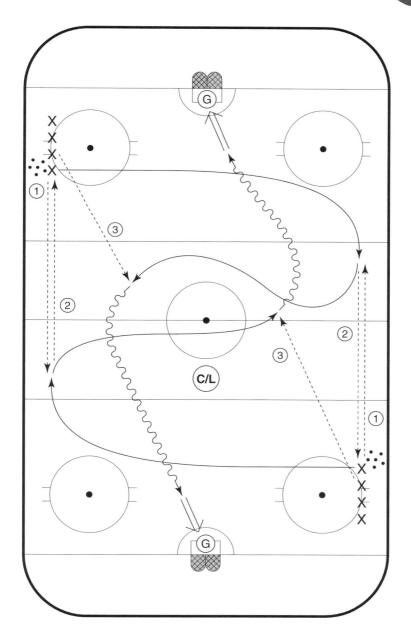

Ranger Drill 53

54 Finland One Touch

Purpose

- Practice one-touch passing while increasing foot speed through the neutral zone

Equipment   None

Time   Three to four minutes

Procedure

1. Players are in the standard four-blues formation (see chapter 5, page 86).
2. At the whistle, one player from each diagonally opposite group skates forward with a puck, then straight-line skates along his or her respective blue line.
3. One-touch passes are made with players from three separate groups as diagrammed. Players generate speed through the neutral zone on the way to the net for a shot on goal.
4. After both players have taken shots to complete the drill, two players from the other groups begin the drill, moving in opposite directions from the first two skaters.

Key Points

- In some cases, the skater might try a deflection pass instead of a direct one-time pass. This is especially true for backhand situations; the skater can simply redirect the puck toward the intended target.

Drill Progressions

- Have players try pivots and 360-degree turns after releasing their passes.
- Players can attempt a one-time shot off the pass to conclude the drill.
- Add a coach who provides a puck from the corner for a second-chance shot.

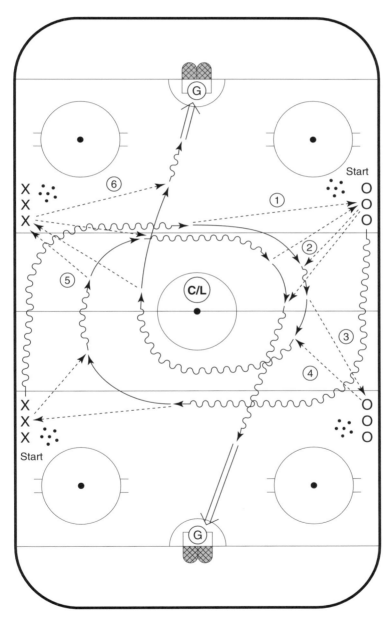

55 Cruise Control

Purpose

- Simulate a transition play through the neutral zone off a one-time pass

Equipment   None

Time   Four to five minutes

Procedure

1. Two equal groups are set up along the sideboards at diagonally opposite sides of the rink near the face-off hash marks.
2. Two players from one group begin the drill. The first player takes a head start to the nearest blue line before the second player starts to skate.
3. Like the Single Wheel drill (see page 62), players skate around the center face-off circle and head back toward the end of the rink where they began.
4. The second skater receives a pass from the opposite line and sends a one-touch pass to his or her partner who shoots on goal, then picks up another puck from the end zone face-off circle.
5. The first skater fires an indirect pass by way of the boards to the second skater who has looped around the center face-off circle. The two complete the drill with a second shot on goal.

Key Points

- This is another drill where timing is essential to effectively execute the one-time pass.
- The lead skater must especially focus on keeping the feet in motion.

Drill Progressions

- Try both corners (four players) going at the same time. Heads up!

Cruise Control

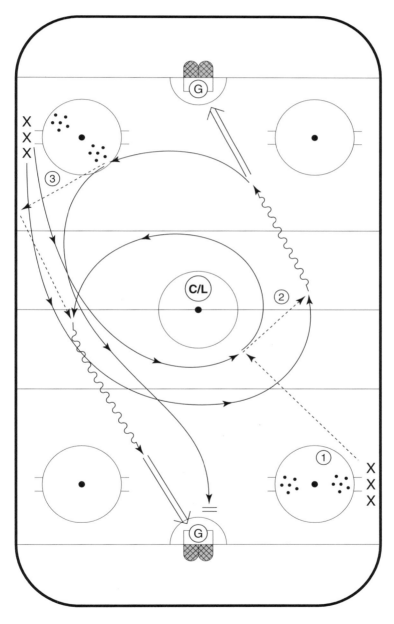

56 Irish One Touch

Purpose

- Reinforce turning skills while introducing one-touch passes from a long distance

Equipment   None

Time   Two to three minutes

Procedure

1. Players are in two groups in diagonally opposite corners of the rink.
2. On the whistle, the first two players from one group skate around both end face-off circles as diagrammed, then begin skating up the ice.
3. As they come out of their turns around the second face-off circle, the next two players in the group send long cross-ice passes to the skaters. The skaters then attempt to send a one-time pass directly to the coach in the neutral zone. The coach returns the puck immediately.
4. The skaters move in for a shot on goal as the whistle sounds for the next players to begin.

Key Points

- The players sending the long passes must stagger these first passes slightly so that the coach does not receive two one-time passes simultaneously.
- The skaters might consider staggering their starts slightly as well to create a gap as they complete the activity with shots on goal.

Drill Progressions

- Make one of the skaters a backchecker, forcing the other skater to attempt a solid one-time pass while under pressure from the backside.

Irish One Touch

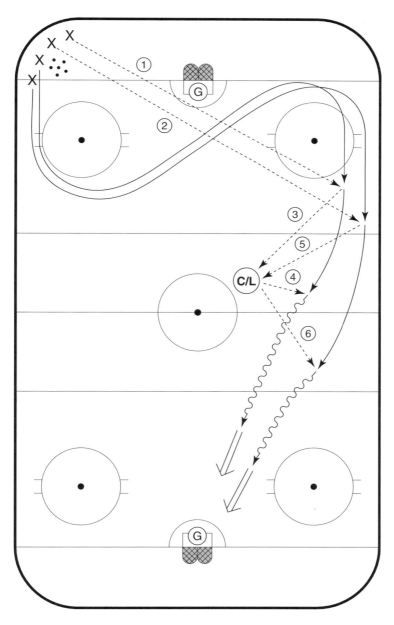

57 Swedish One Touch

Purpose

- Reinforce one-touch passing and receiving

Equipment   None

Time   Two to three minutes

Procedure

1. Players are in the standard four-blues formation (see chapter 5, page 86).
2. Two players with pucks skate forward from diagonally opposite lines (only one skater's route is shown in the diagram). The skaters pivot to backward skating at the blue line and one-time pass and receive while straight-line skating backward along the blue line.
3. Once they reach the far face-off dot, the skaters pivot forward and skate toward the other group at their original end of the ice.
4. The skaters exchange a one-time pass and reception with the closest group. The drill concludes with a shot on goal.
5. As the shots are taken, players from the remaining two lines begin the drill, skating in the opposite directions.

Key Points

- Players should handle the puck as they skate backward, simulating a retreat game situation.
- Players should practice pivoting in both directions.

Drill Progressions

- Add an additional one-time sequence at the beginning of the drill.
- Have a coach include another one-time sequence from the corner toward the end of the drill, thereby increasing the total number of one-time opportunities.

Swedish One Touch

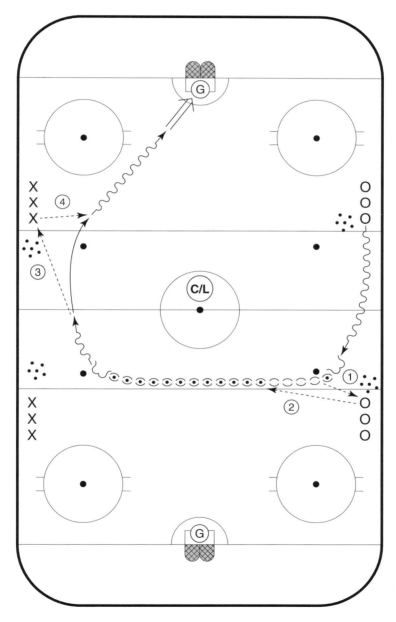

⟨58⟩ Team Canada One Time

Purpose

- Reinforce stationary and moving one-touch passing and receiving

Equipment   None

Time   Three to four minutes

Procedure

1. Players are in four groups, one at each corner of the rink. One player from each group is a designated passer and stands in the neutral zone near one of the face-off dots.
2. On the whistle, one player from diagonally opposite groups passes to the designated passer in the nearest neutral zone, then skates without a puck through the neutral zone as diagrammed.
3. While the skater moves through the neutral zone, the two designated passers practice stationary one-time passing. When the skater is near the center red line, the passer with the puck passes back to the skater.
4. The skater completes the drill with a shot on goal. The next two players from opposite corners begin the drill.

Key Points

- The designated passers should see how many times they can make passes until forced to release the puck to the skater.
- The final pass should be timed so that it is a one-time, cross-ice pass.

Drill Progressions

- Have the players in the neutral zone act as a four-player unit instead of a two-player unit, exchanging passes between all four designated passers as the skaters move through the zone.

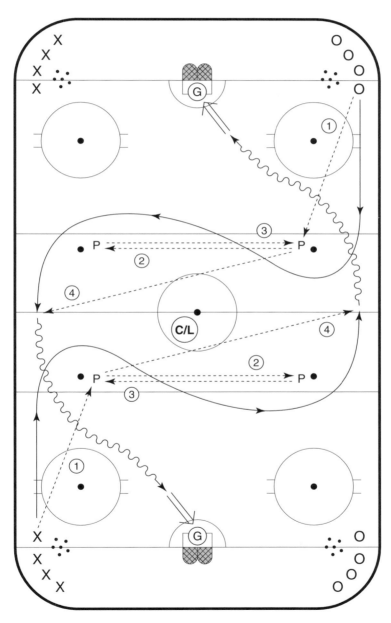

(59) Avalanche

Purpose

- Practice high-speed skating and one-time passing and receiving

Equipment   None

Time   Three to four minutes

Procedure

1. This is a variation of the previous drill (#58) and a cousin of the wheel drills in chapter 4. Players start in the standard four-blues formation (see chapter 5, page 86), except four players stand around the center face-off circle in the neutral zone to serve as designated passers.
2. Diagonally opposite groups begin. One player from each line passes to either designated passer on the far side.
3. The skaters follow a wheel route around the center circle and turn back toward their original end.
4. The designated passers send one-time passes to each other as many times as possible, then pass to the skaters who go in for a shot on goal. After the shot, the remaining two lines begin the drill.

Key Points

- In this drill, the skater receives the outlet pass from a different set of designated passers than in the previous drill.
- Timing is again a key. No offsides are allowed.

Drill Progressions

- Add other one-time passes between the skaters and the first players in the other groups.

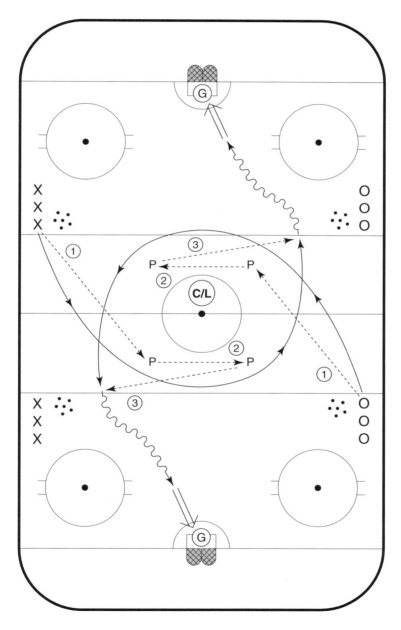

60 Raider One Touch

Purpose

- Practice one-touch passing, timing, and escaping

Equipment   None

Time   Five to six minutes

Procedure

1. Be sure to check the diagram on this one. Forwards are in two groups along opposite sideboards in the neutral zone; defensemen are behind diagonally opposite goal lines.
2. On the whistle, a defenseman from each end skates forward with a puck to the top of the face-off circle. The defenseman pivots and skates backward until reaching the bottom of the circle. He or she then sends a release pass to a forward who has curled into the zone with the defenseman.
3. The defenseman skates as fast as possible toward the other end of the ice, exchanging a one-time pass with the forward on the opposite side of the ice.
4. The defenseman skates into the offensive zone late and receives a pass from the forward who has performed a delayed escape move in the corner. The defenseman takes a one-time shot.

Key Points

- Defensemen must get up the ice as quickly as possible to make the one-touch pass.
- Players must start only on the whistle, as timing is a key factor.

Drill Progressions

- No drill progressions are necessary here.

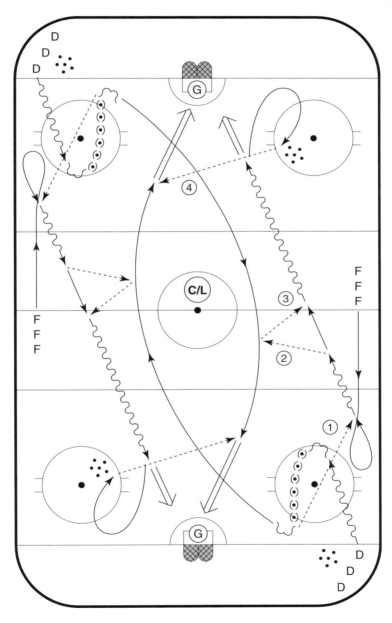

8

Aggressive Timing and Transitions

Picture for a moment Paul Kariya charging up the middle of the ice and honing in on a loose puck, the result of an errant pass. Kariya and other great players from the National Hockey League can turn what initially appears to be an insignificant miscue into a great offensive opportunity because they are prepared to make transitions. With players such as Kariya, Gretzky, Sakic, and Bure, the puck always seems to follow them around the ice; in reality, it is the other way around. These highly skilled players know the value of proper positioning as it relates to opportunity during a game.

By this point, players should have learned all the essential elements that contribute to being an effective passer and receiver. With these foundational skills firmly intact, hang on to your hat (or helmet) because we are about to open things up. Throughout this book, we have referred to *transition play*, a term often poorly defined and misunderstood even in the professional leagues. For our purposes, transition play applies to three different scenarios.

The first situation occurs when a team turns over the puck in their own defensive zone, creating a scoring opportunity for their opponent. Many coaches do not consider this situation a transition play in the purest sense. More coaches are accepting this situation as a transition play, however, especially when the puck is turned over when the team has full possession and has begun to exit their defensive zone.

The second, and potentially most exciting, transition play occurs in or near the neutral zone when the puck is turned over by the opposing team. Players can use this situation to make great gains when they possess the speed and passing skills to execute a high-tempo transition play. Whether initiated by a forward or a defenseman, transition play in the neutral zone can create tremendous excitement and offensive scoring opportunities.

The third transition play can be seen when players enter an opponent's zone. During an offensive rush, teammates often make the faulty assumption that their team has possession of the puck and is about to go on an offensive attack. Problems can develop suddenly if the puck is stripped from a player as the player enters the offensive zone. A weak side defenseman, who only seconds ago was skating hard to support the play as a second wave attacker, must suddenly hustle back to avoid being outnumbered in the defensive zone. Making the transition from offense to defense is often a matter of proper positioning and thinking ahead to avoid problems.

In all of these transitional situations, timing is a critical element. Timing and transition go hand in hand. Whether stretching the neutral zone while looking for a long outlet pass or skating back hard into position for a defensive assignment, good timing in the dynamics of transition improves skills in all phases of this important part of the modern game.

This chapter provides a selection of timing and transition activities designed to move play to a faster tempo. Players may find some of these drills to be frustrating at first, as they struggle with the timing and its impact on effective passing and receiving. Remind them to be patient; this important element of play will improve with practice. Even players who are not the swiftest of foot, however, can benefit from proper positioning and timing to create or take away chances through transition. The puck will always travel faster than even the quickest player, so efficient passing can overcome a multitude of other skill weaknesses. Practicing these drills will help players learn to create better opportunities for scoring during the course of a game.

61 Erik's Loop

Purpose

- Introduce transition play

Equipment None

Time Three to four minutes

Procedure

1. Players are in four groups, two in either corner and two along the sideboards in the neutral zone.
2. A player from one of the neutral zone lines skates toward the nearest face-off circle, then releases a pass to the opposite corner group.
3. After receiving the return pass, the skater circles around and skates with the puck into the neutral zone, passing to the next person in his or her original line.
4. Making sure not to go offside, the skater receives a return pass and skates in for a shot on goal.

Key Points

- Players should rotate in a clockwise direction from one group to the next, making sure to have a turn in each group.
- Time the play so that the puck carrier has plenty of time to receive the second pass before turning up the ice for a quick break on goal.

Drill Progressions

- Include one-touch passing for part or all of the passing sequence (see diagram).
- Designate a defenseman and make it a 1 on 1 into the offensive zone.

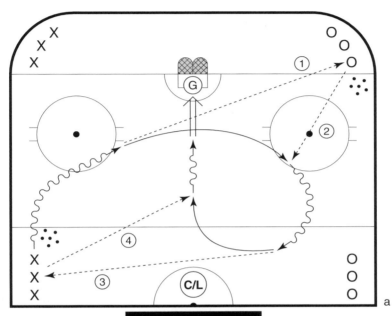

a

Drill Progression

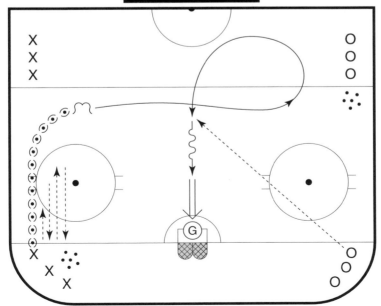

b

62 Kon Man's Delight

Purpose

- Practice timing through the neutral zone during transition opportunities

Equipment None

Time Three to four minutes

Procedure

1. Players are in the standard four-blues formation (see chapter 5, page 86).
2. Players from diagonally opposite lines start at the same time. One receives a pass from the group along the same sideboards. The puck carrier pivots backward and skates backward toward the near blue line, retreating and puck handling all the way.
3. At the same time, the second skater loops near the center red line and then skates back toward the blue line, calling for the puck.
4. The puck carrier skates with the puck beyond the blue line and fires a pass to the other skater, who goes in for a shot on goal.

Key Points

- Timing is key. The player without the puck may have to create space by skating along the blue line to stay onside.
- The puck carrier must time the pass to spring the receiver into a potential breakaway.

Drill Progressions

- Have the passer follow the skater for a second shot opportunity.
- Include another group in the drill and use an additional tip or one-time pass.

Kon Man's Delight

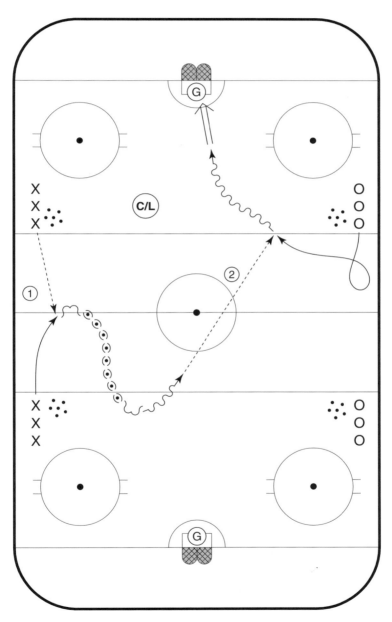

63 Doc's Give and Go

Purpose

- Practice timing and quick transition passing through the neutral zone

Equipment None

Time Two to three minutes

Procedure

1. Players are in four equal groups throughout the neutral zone as diagrammed.
2. At the whistle, one player from each group closest to the center face-off dot circles into the nearest zone below the blue line and receives a pass. (To start the drill, a coach can make the first pass.)
3. At the same time, a player from the group along the sideboards skates toward the far blue line, turns, and begins to sprint toward the opposite end of the ice. Once the sprinting skater passes the blue line, the puck carrier sends a long, two-line pass to the sprinting skater who takes a shot on goal.
4. The shooter continues toward the corner, retrieves a puck from below the goal line and begins the sequence again by passing to a player from the opposite side of the rink.

Key Points

- The players in the neutral zone must time their skating to coincide with the outlet pass from the previous shooter.
- The lead skater must remember to stay onside. Timing is critical.

Drill Progressions

- Have the outlet passer from the corner skate back into the oncoming shooter to provide resistance.
- Create another group and designate a defensive player as a backchecker.

Doc's Give and Go

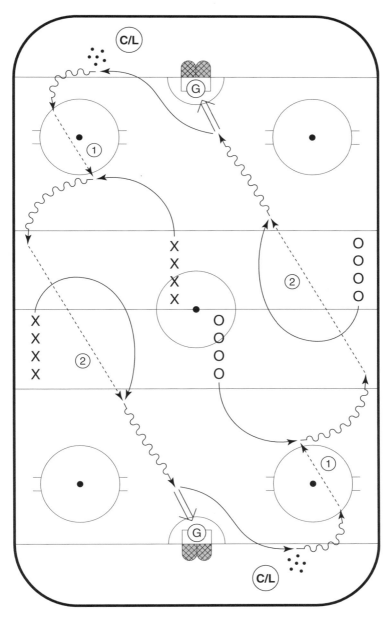

64 Orr's Transition Quickie

Purpose

- Reinforce quick passing and transition opportunities through the neutral zone
- Practice and reinforce the importance of second-wave scoring chances

Equipment None

Time Three to four minutes

Procedure

1. Forwards are in two groups at opposite corners of the rink along the same sideboards; defensemen are in the remaining two corners.
2. One forward skates with a puck into the neutral zone. At the same time, a defenseman from the opposite corner skates without a puck into the neutral zone and receives a pass from the skating forward.
3. Once the defenseman has received the pass, he or she pivots to skate backward and begins to handle the puck.
4. The defenseman sends an outlet pass to the forward who has continued skating through the neutral zone. The forward takes a shot on goal.
5. The defenseman follows into the offensive zone, receives a pass from the coach, and takes a second shot.

Key Points

- The forward must release the puck and generate great speed through the neutral zone.
- The defenseman can pass directly or indirectly off the sideboards.

Drill Progressions

- Use the forward as a screen or deflector for the second shot.
- Use two defensemen. Each must pass once to the other defenseman before releasing to the forward.

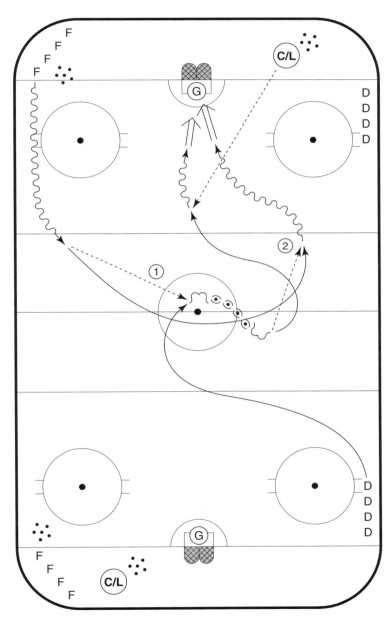

65 Mario's Regroup

Purpose

- Develop transition and escape skills to generate offensive scoring chances

Equipment None

Time Three to four minutes

Procedure

1. Forwards are in two equal groups in both corners at one end of the rink. Defensemen are in groups near the face-off dots in the same end.
2. One defenseman skates backward with a puck to the center red line then skates back toward the blue line. At the same time, a forward skates without a puck following the diagrammed route.
3. Once the forward is across the ice and heading toward the center red line, the defenseman pivots forward and sends a quick outlet pass. The forward takes a shot on goal, gets another puck from the cache behind the goal line, and passes to the defenseman who has joined the attack.
4. Once the defenseman has advanced into the neutral zone, a pair of players in the opposite corner begins.

Key Points

- The defenseman must not only handle the puck while skating backward at high speed but also must remain aware of the forward's position to make an onside pass.

Drill Progressions

- Add backcheckers or another defenseman at the far end of the rink to introduce pressure.

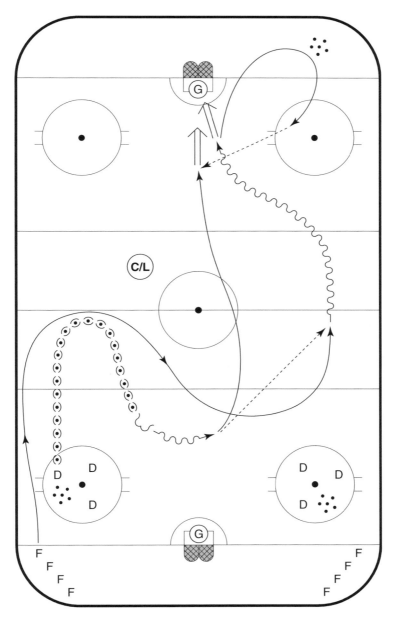

66 Stretch Drill

Purpose

- Practice and refine long passes from the defensive to the neutral zones for quick offensive opportunities

Equipment   None

Time   Two to three minutes

Procedure

1. Players are in two groups in the neutral zone along the sideboards on either side of the center red line as shown.
2. At the whistle, the first player from each line skates toward the closest end zone, then turns and skates along the center red line.
3. To start the sequence, a coach may pass from the corner. The skater receives the pass onside and goes in for a shot.
4. Once the skater takes the shot, the skater retreats into the corner, retrieves a puck, and sends a long pass to the next player who has started the sequence.

Key Points

- The next player in line should begin skating as the puck receiver crosses the center red line.
- The player who makes the pass from the corner may also try an indirect pass off the boards, rather than always going tape to tape.

Drill Progressions

- Have two players skate through the neutral zone and have one attempt a tip or a one-time pass.

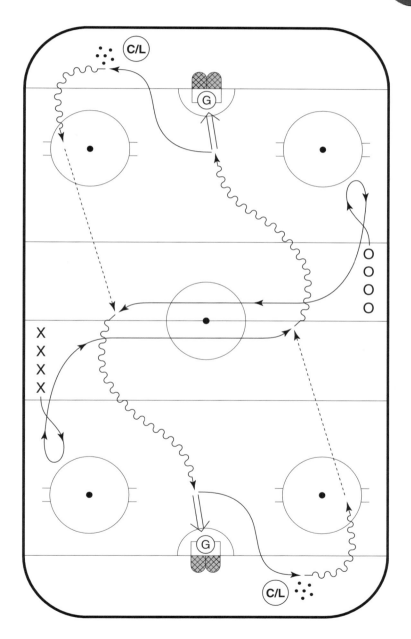

(67) Thunder Bay Stretch 2 on 0

Purpose

- Practice long lead passes through the middle of the neutral zone for breakaway opportunities

Equipment   None

Time   Two to three minutes

Procedure

1. Players are in two groups at diagonally opposite corners of the rink.
2. At the whistle, the first player in each group skates quickly along the sideboards, curls toward the middle of the ice in the far zone, and accepts a pass from the opposite corner.
3. After a slight delay, the second player in each line skates forward. He or she turns in the neutral zone and moves across the ice through the zone.
4. The first skater takes the puck into the neutral zone and makes a long lead pass to the breaking second skater who goes for a shot on goal. After the shot, the shooter retrieves a puck from below the goal line for the next pair involved in the sequence.

Key Points

- A coach may begin the passing sequence from the corner for the first pair of skaters. Thereafter, however, the shooter must remember to make the outlet pass.
- Timing, timing, timing!

Drill Progressions

- Have the neutral zone passer follow for a second shot on goal.
- Have the passer from the corner backcheck and battle the neutral zone passer for a loose puck provided by a coach along the sideboards.

Thunder Bay Stretch 2 on 0

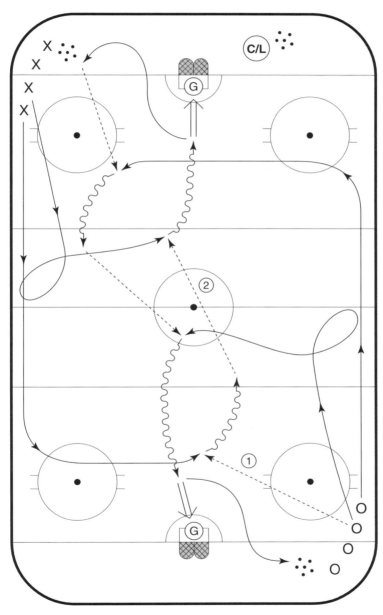

171

68 Timing 3 on 0

Purpose

- Condition players through a timing and passing drill
- Reinforce proper breadth and width into the neutral and offensive zones

Equipment   None

Time   Five to six minutes

Procedure

1. Players are in four equal groups in the four corners of the rink. Members from three of the four groups will be used in each attack sequence.
2. One player from one end of the rink skates along the length of the ice, cuts through the middle of the zone, and receives a pass from a player in the opposite diagonal corner.
3. As the first player receives the pass, two additional players from the same end and corner of the rink join the attack up ice, making this a 3-on-0 activity, and completing the drill with a shot on goal at the original skater's end of the ice.
4. As the three players exit the far zone, a single skater from one of the far groups begins the sequence again toward the opposite end of the ice.

Key Points

- This drill provides an opportunity for players to be creative offensively while airing out the skates.
- All participants should be going at top-end speed. No coasting allowed.

Drill Progressions

- Have the three players complete a minimum number of passes before shooting.
- Add a chaser who will backcheck the player of his or her choice.

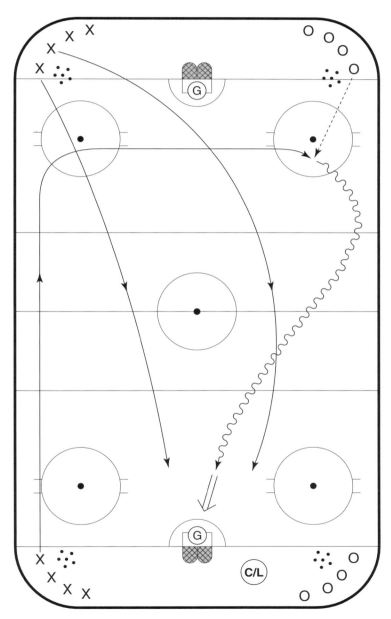

⟨69⟩ Buccaneer 3 on 0

Purpose

- Practice long passes through the neutral zone and high-speed change of direction
- Add a conditioning factor

Equipment None

Time Five to six minutes

Procedure

1. Players are in four groups in the four corners of the rink.
2. The first players in both groups at one end of the rink skate forward. One player has a puck, the other does not.
3. The skaters exchange two long, cross-ice passes before passing to the first player in a group at the other end. As they are making the pass to the corner, the two skaters switch places by skating across the ice.
4. A return pass is made from the corner, and the passer joins the original two skaters, making this a full-ice 3 on 0.

Key Points

- As the first group vacates the zone, the next pair begins in the opposite direction.
- High tempo is key as players are working on conditioning as well as passing and transition.

Drill Progressions

- Add another player and make it a 4-on-0 drill.
- Use two players as backcheckers only, making this a high-tempo, high-pressure drill.

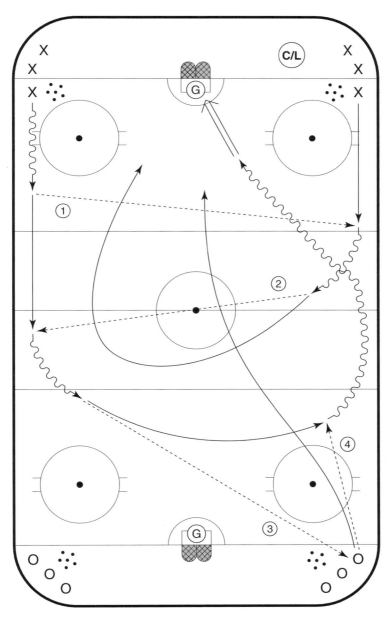

70 Redhawk 4 on 0

Purpose

- Have offensive fun while working on passing and conditioning

Equipment   None

Time   Five to six minutes

Procedure

1. Players are in two groups along the same sideboards in the neutral zone. A designated passer or a coach waits in the corner next to a cache of pucks.
2. At the whistle, four players from one group skate into different breakout positions and prepare to skate toward the opposite end of the rink. One of the four must turn and pivot near the closest sideboard while the other three move into open ice away from the boards.
3. The designated passer or coach sends an outlet pass to any of the four skaters, who proceed toward the other end in a 4-on-0 play.
4. Once a shot is taken, the other group sends four players in the opposite direction.

Key Points

- Stretch the passing possibilities by having the skaters move into as many areas as possible. The four skaters should never be bunched together during this drill.
- The passer from the corner may pass early or late. The four skaters must time their reactions.

Drill Progressions

- Have the four players complete a shot and then go back to the other end to receive a puck for a second shot on goal.

Redhawk 4 on 0

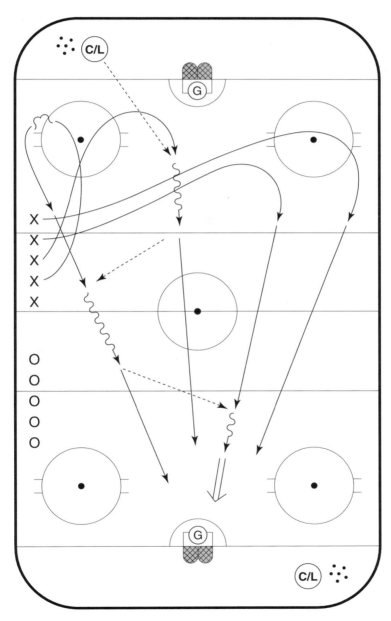

Mastery of Passing and Receiving

If you have been practicing all the drills presented in this book, we anticipate that by now your own or your players' passing and receiving skills have improved greatly. To test these improved skills, this chapter provides unique drills to use as a measuring stick of passing and receiving mastery. By now, players should feel comfortable with both forehand and backhand mechanics, be able to make or receive a pass at high speed, and possess the ability to execute the skill set under pressure in game conditions.

The drills in this chapter will test even the most gifted players when it comes to their passing and receiving prowess. Many of the drills are extremely difficult overload activities that force players to focus on the task at hand. Given time and sufficient practice, players will be able to complete the majority of these tasks with all the skill of a master player. In the short term, remember that passing and receiving, like all skill components in hockey, take years to refine. Patience and determination are required to overcome the initial struggle on the road to mastery.

Good luck, and, as always, "keep your stick on the ice!"

ⓐ Long Leads

Purpose

- Refine long-lead passing and receiving, timing, and finishing skills

Equipment   None

Time   Three to five minutes

Procedure

1. Players begin in four equal groups in the four corners of the rink.
2. One player from each of the two groups at one end of the rink skates forward. A coach passes to one of the skaters.
3. The receiver quickly relays a long-lead pass to the other skater, who, after receiving the puck, continues the length of the ice for a shot on goal.
4. The initial receiver continues to skate forward and loops back toward the starting end of the rink while the shooter loops toward the same end and receives a second puck from another coach. The puck carrier sends a long-lead pass to his or her partner, who takes a second shot on goal.
5. Once both skaters have cleared the far offensive zone, a pair of players from that end begins the drill in the opposite direction.

Key Points

- Players must remember to keep all passes onside and time their turns so that the second pass is executed successfully at top speed.

Drill Progressions

- This is all the drill you need! Make sure it is done at top-end speed.

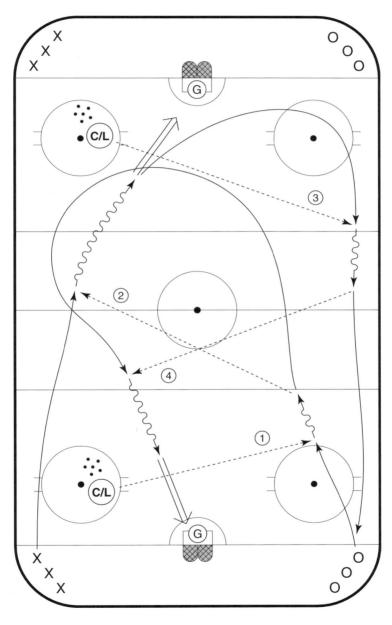

72 Swing Daddy

Purpose

- Enhance foot speed, timing, and passing skills at a high tempo

Equipment None

Time Two to three minutes

Procedure: Half-Ice Drill

1. Players are located as diagrammed with three groups equally distributed in the neutral and offensive zones.
2. A player in the neutral zone near the sideboards skates without a puck toward the front of the net. A player from the corner group sends a pass that is one-timed back.
3. The first player in the corner group skates forward with a puck after the initial skater has gone by and feeds a short pass to that skater.
4. A give-and-go pass exchange (see drill #36) is completed with the middle group. The puck carrier goes in for a shot on goal to complete the drill. The corner passer moves to the net to catch any rebounds.

Key Points

- Players must rotate to every group to practice both stationary and moving passing and receiving from all different angles.
- Once a player starts skating, the speed should increase, not decrease, as the drill progresses.

Drill Progressions

- Start with a puck and take a one-time shot off the one-time pass at the front end of the drill.
- Add a stationary defenseman at the blue line or a forward behind the net to provide a second-shot opportunity.

Swing Daddy

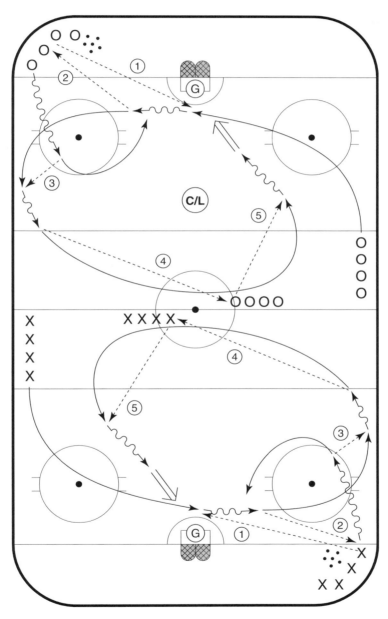

73 Continuous Traction 2 on 1

Purpose

- Reinforce quick transition passes from defense to offense

Equipment   None

Time   Five to six minutes

Procedure: Full-Ice Drill

1. Forwards are in equal groups in all four corners with defensemen in two equal groups at diagonally opposite ends of the rink.
2. Two forwards, one from each group at one end of the rink, and one defenseman from the same end skate forward, then move back toward their original end. The defenseman pivots and skates backward.
3. As the forwards turn at the far blue line, a defenseman from the other end passes to the nearest forward who relays the pass to the other forward.
4. A 2 on 1 ensues, with the puck given up to the defenseman just inside the blue line. The defenseman feeds the puck to another pair of forwards who have started the drill going the opposite way.
5. A coach supplies another puck to the original forwards to complete the drill with a shot on goal.

Key Points

- The entire drill requires only one puck to pass through the neutral zone between forwards and defensemen.
- Timing is key as the defensemen must take the puck, pivot forward, and work the transition pass at full speed.

Drill Progressions

- Add a third forward or second defenseman to increase the passing options during transition.

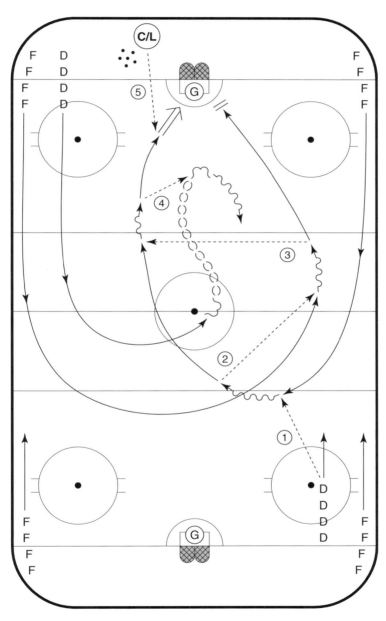

74 One-Time Charlie

Purpose

- Practice carrying and passing the puck out of the defensive zone

Equipment None

Time Five minutes

Procedure: Full-Ice Drill

1. Forwards and defensemen are located in separate groups in the neutral zone as diagrammed.
2. The first forward dumps the puck into the defensive zone. At the same time, a defenseman skates backward, then pivots to pick up the loose puck for a breakout pass.
3. As the defenseman gains possession of the puck, the forward loops out of the zone, receiving a pass through the middle and immediately one-time returning it to the defenseman.
4. The forward continues skating up the ice as the defenseman carries the puck to the blue line and makes a crisp, neutral zone pass to the breaking forward who finishes with a shot on goal.

Key Points

- Forwards must delay their loop out of the neutral zone, or the first pass from the defenseman will be difficult to handle. Timing is important.
- The forward should try and stretch the pass as far as possible in the neutral zone. If necessary, the forward may have to straight-line skate along the far blue line to keep the pass onside.

Drill Progressions

- Have the defensemen pivot and play a 1 on 1 with the forward from the opposite group.
- Have the defensemen follow up ice for a second shot opportunity at the other end.

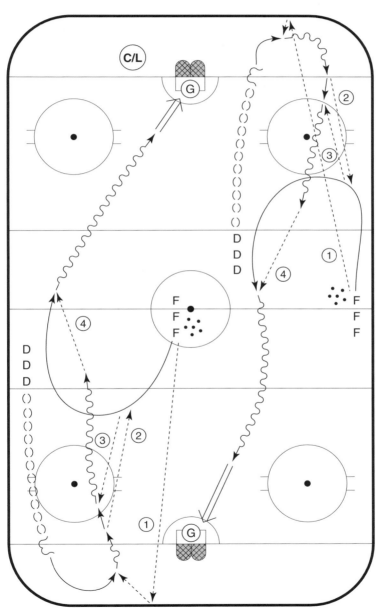

75 Tylenol 7

Purpose

- Reinforce excellent passing and receiving skills at a high tempo

Equipment None

Time Four to five minutes

Procedure: Full-Ice Drill

1. Although the diagram may appear to show a half-ice drill, groups in the neutral zone are used for both ends during this activity. Forwards and defensemen are split and located as diagrammed.
2. The first forward from each group along the sideboards in the neutral zone passes a puck to the defenseman directly in front of him or her. The forward then skates the route as diagrammed.
3. The defenseman skates backward with the puck to the goal line, pivots forward, and passes off the end boards to the corner group, which relays the puck to the forward in motion.
4. The forward then exchanges a one-time pass and reception sequence with the other neutral zone line then does the same with his or her original group.
5. The forward completes the drill with a shot on goal.

Key Points

- Players must be alert, whether at the front or back of a line, because passes are coming fast and furious, some in rapid succession.

Drill Progressions

- Have the defenseman step up into the play and create a 1 on 1.
- Have the forward in the corner come into the play as a deflector or rebounder.

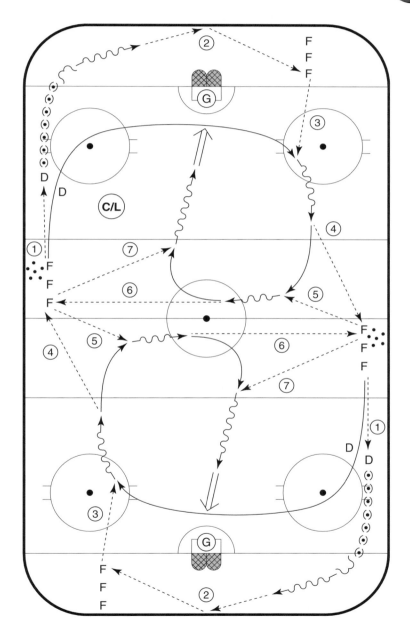

Sample Practice Sessions

The following sample practice plans will give coaches ideas on structuring practices using the activities in this book. Establish themes for each practice so that players know what is expected of them, and link objectives to the theme for that practice. Often, coaches include drills and activities that, by themselves, might be valuable toward skill development. Be sure to explain the main objective to players, however, so they can focus on success. Intense focus on improving certain skill sets increases success in a shorter period of time.

When designing an effective practice session, consider the following important factors.

• *Take time to prepare.* Have a general game plan for each practice and share the theme and objectives with coaches, volunteers, and players. Subthemes should fall within the main objectives, flowing nicely from the day's drills. Notice that in passing and receiving practices, the main theme relates to the specific skill set of passing and receiving. Subthemes build upon those skills. Whatever the plan, always take the time to prepare. Spend a few moments sharing ideas with players before hitting the ice.

• *Use the entire ice surface and available time efficiently.* Rather than running full-ice drills, split the ice in halves, thirds, or quarters, depending on the lesson theme. Ice time costs can be prohibitive, so it is important to make every second count. Many of the drills in this book are full ice, but they can be modified easily to fit half-ice or station methods.

• *Break the team into workable groups.* Keep players active for as much of the time as is possible. Running a full-ice drill with only two active players while 18 others stand around doing nothing is not inclusive or efficient. Break the team into small groups so players can repeat each drill more often.

• *Consider station work to reinforce specific skills.* Station-based learning is a popular concept. If the overall theme is individual passing and receiving development, divide the team into pairs or groups placed at specific drill stations. Design a variety of activities that develop aspects of passing and receiving. Many of the drills in this book can be adapted to station work.

Three-Station Drill Session

The following example demonstrates the use of stations to practice passing and receiving using a three-station drill. Station work is fun and reinforces basic passing and receiving skills effectively. Players will quickly understand the organization and sequence they must follow.

In the following example, we describe the individual stations and flow of the drilling pattern as well. Be creative and try station work as an effective way of drilling a hockey team.

Guidelines for Three-Station Drills

- Split ice lengthwise into thirds, marking the boundaries for each station with pylons (see figure A). Split the team into thirds, with each group going to one station.
- An extra net can be brought on the ice for drills that finish with a shot on goal. (However, shooting does not have to be included to complete a drill.)
- Players go through the station and return to the same line, *making sure not to cross into another lane* (a dangerous, high-speed collision could occur).
- Players return to the line by staying tight to the pylon boundary markers, making certain not to interfere with the next person doing the drill.
- Ensure that players understand how each station is run. Demonstrate the activity if possible.
- On the whistle, groups rotate to the next station.
- Total time per station is approximately 5 minutes; the entire activity will take 15 to 17 minutes.

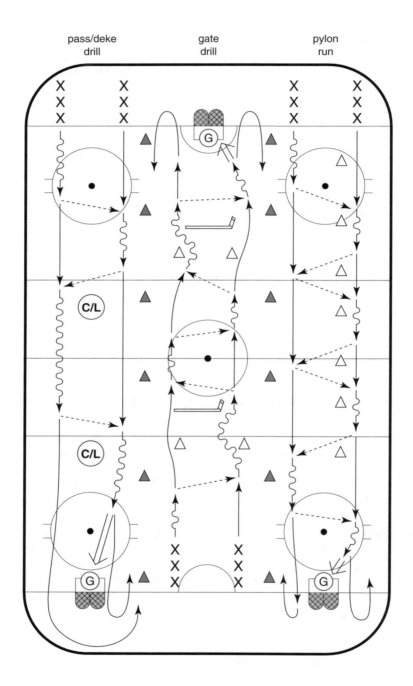

Pass or Deke Drill

Put a leader or coach at each blue line to force oncoming players to maneuver by either passing or dekeing. The blue line player may skate laterally only. Depending on age and skill level, restrict contact, perhaps allowing only stick checking for younger participants.

Gate Drill

Put two pylons about five feet apart at one blue line with a hockey stick on the ice about three to five feet directly behind them. Set up a similar "gate" at the other blue line. Players exchange passes as they skate toward the pylons. The player with the puck skates through the pylons and cuts sharply in either direction around the stick. The skaters continue to exchange passes until the next gate where the sequence is done again. If possible, have someone stand behind the gate and point in either direction as the players approach. The players must react quickly and go in the direction indicated. Make the drill more demanding by moving the stick closer to the gate, making the cut more extreme. Again, this depends on the team's skill level.

Pylon Run

Set pylons far apart, then have a series of three or four close together, forcing players to make quick passes as they skate forward. If players are on their backhand side, then backhand passes must be made. Once the players are at the red line, the next pair in line may begin.

Sample Practice Plans

The following examples demonstrate applying one common theme—improving passing and receiving skills—in a variety of ways using different objectives and subthemes. Remember when designing practice plans that a drill from one topic can be substituted for another part of practice. Experiment with different combinations and seek feedback about the effectiveness of a particular practice. Learn and try new ideas. The perfect practice might be just around the corner!

For the following practices, add an extra 5 minutes for transition time between drills. Remember that most arena facilities allot 10 minutes each hour to resurface the ice.

SAMPLE PRACTICE PLAN ONE

Total Time: 60 minutes
Theme: Passing and receiving
Objective: To refine foundational passing and receiving skills

Drill Sequence	Time Required (min)
1. **Drill #16—Mason Partner Pass** *An effective, simple warm-up activity.*	4
2. **Drill #4—Pepper** *Will loosen arms, wrists, and hands.*	4
3. **Drill #20—Leamington Warm-Up** *Get the legs moving while preparing goalies as well.*	4
4. **Drill #22—2-on-0 Wheel** *Add a change of direction at higher speeds.*	5
5. **Drill #24—Delayed Wheel** *A variation and progression based on drill #22.*	3
6. **Drill #48—Indirect Break** *Add a subtheme of indirect breakouts.*	5
7. **Drill #50—Pass Conditioner** *Take some time to pass and condition, too.*	10
8. **Drill #70—Redhawk 4 on 0** *Finish practice on a high note with a fun activity.*	5
9. **Recap, optional skate at the end, or a controlled passing and receiving scrimmage**	5

Total Activity Time   45

SAMPLE PRACTICE PLAN TWO

Total Time: 60 minutes

Theme: Passing, receiving, and an introduction to transition

Objective: Refine passing and receiving through transitions

Drill Sequence	Time Required (min)
1. Drill #5—Self-Serve *Warm-up; players work on accuracy and touch.*	**5**
2. Drill #8—Escalator *Players pass the puck while skating both forward and backward.*	**5**
3. Drill #13—Swing Warm-Up *Finish with shots on goal to warm up goalies, too.*	**5**
4. Drill #21—Single Wheel *Really gets the blood flowing.*	**5**
5. Drill #25—Six-Pass Wheel *Continuation of drill #21 with more passes, more challenge.*	**5**
6. Drill #39—2-on-0 Delay *A solid introductory activity for the concept of timing.*	**5**
7. Drill #62—Kon Man's Delight *Emphasize a simple transition idea for the neutral zone.*	**5**
8. Showdown (1-on-1 play with goalie from center ice) and some 3-on-3 scrimmage play *This is always a great way to finish any practice.*	**10**

Total Activity Time	45

SAMPLE PRACTICE PLAN THREE

Total Time: 60 minutes

Theme: Passing and receiving

Objective: Develop passing and receiving skills under time and space restrictions

Drill Sequence	Time Required (min)
1. Drill #12—Stop-and-Go Passing and Receiving *Warm-up and emphasize accuracy while passing.*	4
2. Drill #9—Full-Ice Reverse *An easy adaptation of drill #12.*	4
3. Drill #28—Two-Puck Exchange *Passing and receiving with speed; getting goalies involved.*	5
4. Drill #40—Double Escape *Introduce time and space pressure.*	5
5. Drill #60—Raider One Touch *High speed and little time to execute a difficult one-time tip pass.*	5
6. Drill #66—Stretch Drill *Stretch it, but don't run out of real estate.*	5
7. Drill #73—Continuous Traction 2 on 1 *This high-speed drill will test any age group.*	8
8. Drill #23—Situation Wheel *Work on various outmanned situations into the offensive zone.*	6
9. Cool down and stretch at center ice *Recap key teaching points during this time.*	3

Total Activity Time	45

About Huron Hockey School

Hockey has improved dramatically over the past three decades, and Huron Hockey School, founded in 1970, has matched the sport's progression stride for stride as the leader in hockey instruction, both on the ice and in the classroom.

The Huron curriculum—annually updated and expanded and now including roller hockey—is used internationally from Casper, Wyoming, to Windsor, Ontario, on over 50 campuses, including residential schools in Traverse City, Michigan; Stroudsburg, Pennsylvania; and Toronto and Cornwall, Ontario.

The seeds of Huron's dynamic growth can be traced to the hockey revolution begun in 1970, when Bobby Orr became the first defenseman in National Hockey League history to win the league scoring title. While Orr's Boston Bruins went on to win the Stanley Cup Trophy, three young coaches realized the need for a more scientific approach to teaching the fundamentals of the sport they loved.

From the analytical minds of Ron Mason (now the all-time most winning coach in collegiate hockey), Bill Mahoney (former head coach of the Minnesota North Stars), and Brian Gilmour (an All-American at Boston University in 1967), evolved a now time-tested philosophy of hockey instruction by "professional educators." Huron is made up of people who know how to *teach* the game and who know the nuances that make a hockey instructor most effective. This concept of teaching hockey fundamentals has benefited more than 150,000 players, including over 500 who have made it to the National Hockey League. In addition, 60 Huron instructors have moved through the coaching ranks into the world's greatest league.

Hockey has truly become a global sport, and Huron has become a global hockey school—one that prides itself on making its participants better players. International exchanges have taken Huron staff members to Russia, where in 1965, Ron Mason studied under the legendary coach Anatoli Tarasov, the father of Soviet hockey. Today, the school regularly welcomes youngsters from Japan, Italy, Sweden, Finland, Holland, Germany, Austria, and France, who all come to learn hockey "the Huron way."

Paul O'Dacre
Chief Operating Officer, Huron Hockey School

About the Authors

George Gwozdecky

Vern Stenlund

George Gwozdecky has a winning touch. As head coach at the University of Denver he has once again turned a losing program into a nationally respected contender, just as he had done at Miami University. Gwozdecky is highly regarded as one of hockey's top coaches and most gifted clinic speakers. He also was a top collegiate player at the University of Wisconsin and in 1994 was inducted into the Wisconsin Hockey Hall of Fame. Gwozdecky lives in Denver, Colorado.

K. Vern Stenlund is a leading hockey instructor who played professionally and has coached at all levels. He is also a consultant to the Huron Hockey School and has assisted in establishing satellite clinics in West Orange, New Jersey; Chicago and Geneva, Illinois; Toronto, Ontario; Traverse City, Michigan; and Jackson, Wyoming. Stenlund lives in Windsor, Ontario.

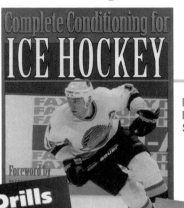
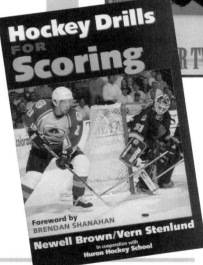
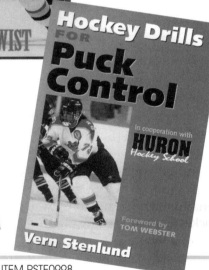